Liberating Genius:
A Framework For Epic Transformation

Liberating Genius:
A Framework For Epic Transformation

Angela Maiers & Mark Moran

Angela Maiers is also the co-author with Amy Sandoval of *Passion Driven Classroom* and author of *Classroom Habitudes*.

Choose2Matter, Inc.
205 Sherman St.
Lynbrook, NY 11563

Choose2Matter.org

Ordering Information:

Special discounts are available on purchases of 25 or more copies. For this or any other special order, contact the publisher at YouMatter@Choose2Matter.org

Dedication

To Genius Everywhere.
We see you.
We value you.
You Matter to the world.

Contents

Acknowledgements

Sincere and special thanks to all the teachers and leaders who on a daily basis make it their business to liberate the genius of all who grace their presence. It is your passion, dedication and commitment that motivated and inspired these lessons.

We have written and rewritten every page of this book with you in mind. A very special thanks to Tammy Dunbar, seeing the lessons come alive in your classroom was beyond anything we dreamed of.

Courtney Collins for your incredible willingness to jump in and join us on this journey. You have an amazing heart.

To our families, the joy of our lives, you astonish us.

And to each of you, our readers, who we have tried to imagine not only reading this book, but using YOUR genius to make it come alive in ways we could not have imagined.

You are already making a difference; whether you know it or not, and the more you understand the difference you are making, the bigger difference it will be.

Angela and Mark

Preface – Why This Book?

Four years ago, I dreamed out loud for school to be a place that honors student passion and genius, and puts it to work for the world.

Wondering boldly:

- *What would happen if students were given sufficient opportunity, encouragement and guidance to discover and explore their passions?*

- *What if all students understood that they have particular aptitudes, perspectives, and passions, and that what makes them "different" is their greatest gift?*

- *What would this mean for their confidence and boldness? For student engagement? For their perceptions about learning and school?*

- *More importantly, what would it mean for the world?*

I imagined a classroom where passion driven genius work was not extracurricular, but was a part of the routine. Students would be invited and expected to collaborate to support each other's genius; to experiment with ideas, discover new possibilities, and make epic things happen.

A few years and a few thousand classrooms later, this dream is becoming a reality. We have conclusive evidence that when we create a time and space for our students to strive audaciously and connect and collaborate with others, their genius is liberated, and learning, lives and worlds change.

Still, we are in the early days of figuring out the best way to turn our classrooms into places of inquiry and experimentation in which pushing limits, discovery and creation are daily activities.

Let's do this together, step-by-step, one lesson at a time and watch our brave grow! I can't wait to take this journey with you!

You Matter,

Angela Maiers

How to Use This Guide

A rose by any other name....

There are many names used for when teachers allocate a certain amount of time each week to allow students to find and explore their passion. Genius Time, 20% Time, and Passion Projects are just a few of them. Because Genius Hour is the most commonly used, and for the sake of consistency, this is the term we will use throughout this book.

How much time must we allocate to Genius Hour?

You will allocate whatever time your classroom schedule permits. It may be a day a week, an hour a day, an hour a week, or it may vary from week to week. We do encourage you to create a steady schedule for the first 20 days, but after many students will work independently, and hopefully, often on their own time!

This book is designed to be useful to a broad range of educators. *Liberating Genius* was initially published in an eBook format filled with links to videos, blogs and articles to support the reader's understanding. The websites are included in this book, but if you wish to access the eBook, you can download it for free here:
http://www.choose2matter.org/liberatinggenius/
At the end of each chapter, there are discussion questions for educators; they can be used to contextualize your thinking while engaging

either with a group or independently. Those of you who are new to Genius Hour or passion-based learning may want to immerse yourselves in each step. Those of you with some experience with Genius Hour may focus your attention on select chapters.

My aim was to make this a one-stop resource for Genius Hour. My lessons only extend 20 days, and seek to set the conditions for a successful launch of Genius Hour. They do not delve deeply into the "output" of Genius Hour - student projects that demonstrate their learning and growing. That I leave to the robust, prolific and generous community of Genius Hour educators who have much to offer you. Thus I've included many helpful resources from other Genius Hour leaders, and suggest some additional reading at the end of the guide.

Genius Hour is not merely a "program" during which students do fun projects. Rather, Genius Hour is a nearly unprecedented opportunity for teachers to guide students in *how* to be effective learners and citizens, by helping them connect what they do in school to the broader community.

By its nature, Genius Hour is flexible, reactive, ever changing, and quite messy. Writing this book and compiling the outside resources was a challenge. I wanted to include enough structure to set you firmly down the path, but every teacher and student will require something a little different from *his or her* Genius Hour.

Be courageous. Be relentless. Be passionate.

The world will demand the same of your students.

Leave No Genius Behind

"The world is always ready to receive talent with open arms. Very often it does not know what to do with genius."

Oliver Wendell Holmes, Sr. Physician and Poet

Stand up if you're a genius.

Are you standing? Would your students be?

It's an interesting experiment to try. Stand in a room of adults, or even teenagers, and ask each genius in the room to rise and be noticed.

I'll caution you ahead of time; you will likely find that you are the only one standing.

Now try the same thing with a group of five-year olds. This time, my warning is more emphatic: move out of the way or be trampled as they charge forward with speed and audacity that will take your breath away. It is amazing to witness.

Why is this? When do we give up ownership of our gifts? Become modest about our talent? Hide our uniqueness? Deny our genius?

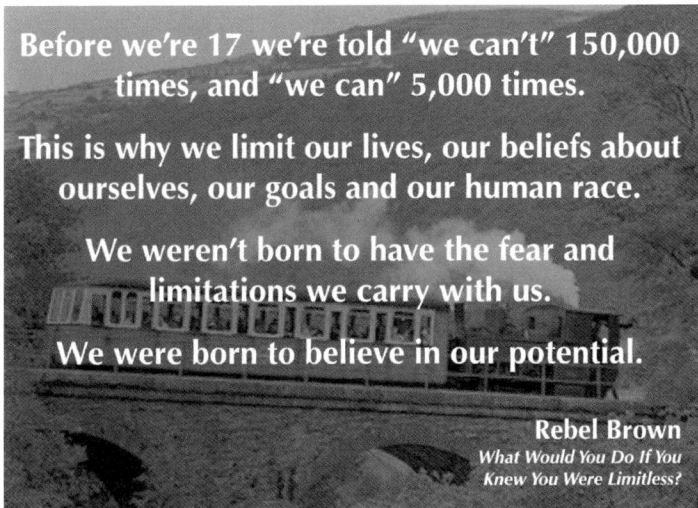

Before we're 17 we're told "we can't" 150,000 times, and "we can" 5,000 times.

This is why we limit our lives, our beliefs about ourselves, our goals and our human race.

We weren't born to have the fear and limitations we carry with us.
We were born to believe in our potential.

Rebel Brown
What Would You Do If You Knew You Were Limitless?

The problem goes beyond this "negative programming." We've pushed students over and over and over again to color inside the lines, fill in the blanks, and answer our questions, and their genius gets left behind.

The result? Too many of our children - and adults too - do carry fear and limitations. We believe that we're not enough.

We have to change that belief. Right here, right now.

Let's scream from the mountaintops the message that the human brain is marvelously plastic, and packs enormous potential -- we just need to tap into it.

Let's change the conversation and put genius on the agenda.

It begins with a new definition and perspective; one that embraces what geniuses do, rather than who and what they are. Let's look beyond IQ, genetic anomalies, and worldwide acclaim and consider the work of genius.

What does a genius do?

I love the list in Seth Godin's book, *Linchpin*:

1. A genius solves a problem in a way no one else could.
2. A genius looks a problem with fresh eyes.
3. A genius changes the rules.
4. A genius is someone who's willing to do the work of a human being,
5. A genius is ready make a unique impact on the world; solve a problem in a new way.
6. A genius gives the world something it didn't know was missing.

Know anyone like this? You do if you teach kindergarten.

In a June 1963 speech to the Parliament of Ireland, President John F. Kennedy proclaimed that, "The problems of the world cannot possibly be solved by skeptics or cynics whose horizons are limited by the obvious realities. We need men who can dream of things that never were and ask - why not?"

This is true now more than ever: our world demands minds that generate new perspectives, seek solutions, and discover emerging opportunities. These are the minds of many students sitting in your classroom today. They may be students who, at first glance, do not let their genius shine through, but I invite you to take a second look at the individuals who we have the privilege of ushering in this new world.

We are in the presence of genius every day. We bear witness to five year olds who know how to finger-paint without stress. Second graders who know how to make you laugh on the dimmest of days. Middle school students brave enough to share their story in front of other people. Children who, if invited and indeed challenged to do so, would give our world something it badly needs.

The education of our children is about leading this genius into the world. Noticing, delighting in, and supporting this genius are at the heart of our work as parents and teachers, to function effectively and gracefully within it.

The ability of our students to lead their best lives depends on our willingness and ability to:

- Notice and honor their genius
- Value and respect their contribution
- Tell them they matter, and are essential to us and the world

When we do all three, we show them we believe in their genius. What follows will take your breath away.

It starts with this sentence:

YOU ARE A GENIUS AND THE WORLD NEEDS YOUR CONTRIBUTION.
ANGELA MAIERS

Imagine if your day started with these words when you walked into school, a staff meeting, or your office.

- How would you feel?
- How would you perform?
- How would that impact others around you?

For students in the classrooms I discuss below, this sign is not just a motivational tool; it is a call to action. Owning their genius is a responsibility they take very seriously, and it shows.

Mrs. Sigler's First Grade Class

At first, Mrs. Sigler's 1st graders thought genius was probably a smart, cute, kind scientist, but they were not exactly sure. They decided to check out how the rest of the world defined 'genius'. They found words like curious, playful, imaginative, innovative, passionate, persistent, joyful and inventive.

All things they aspired to and were willing to become better at. She then asked her kids to tell their fellow classmates and the world why they were geniuses.

Here is what they proclaim that they are willing and ready to contribute:

Brooke

"I am a genius because I am an artist. I am cute. The world needs me to love them."

Ben

"I am a genius because I recycle. The world needs me to help keep the world clean."

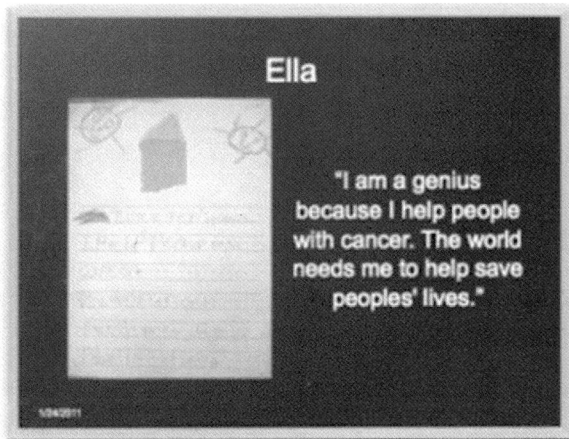

Ella

"I am a genius because I help people with cancer. The world needs me to help save peoples' lives."

Mrs. Jones' Fourth Grade Class

Students in Mrs. Jones, 4th grade class, created the following checklist of Genius Habitudes to work towards and set goals around.

- **Courage**. It takes courage to do things others consider impossible. Stop worrying about what people will think if you're different.
- **Self-Awareness.** Geniuses know what they want and go after it. Get control of your life and schedule. Have something specific to accomplish each day
- **Adaptability**. Being flexible enables you to adapt to changing circumstances readily. Resist doing things the same old way. Be willing to consider new options.
- **Curiosity**. An inquisitive, curious mind will help you seek out new information. Don't be afraid to admit you don't know it all. Always ask questions about things you don't understand.
- **Imagination**. Geniuses know how to think in new combinations, see things from a different perspective, than anyone else. Unclutter your mental environment to develop this type of imagination. Give yourself time each day to daydream, to fantasize, to drift into a dreamy inner life the way you did as a child.
- **Passion and Drive**. Geniuses have a strong desire to work hard and long. They're willing to give all they've got to a project.

Develop your drive by focusing on your future success, and keep going. They not only own their own genius; they are aware of and value the genius of those around them.

Mrs. Voyle's Seventh Grade Class

I love how the 7th graders in Mrs. Voyle's class describe how genius fuels their learning and work:

"Our **genius** calls us to take on **challenges**. Facing those challenges, we acquire the **disciplines** to pursue our work in the world. In doing so we build our **character** and become the **authorities** we are meant to become. It feels like love."

Mrs. Voyle shared her reflection and impact on the study of genius on her blog:

"I have known that the language that I use with my students is so very important and today using these labels really worked for me. I have a student who has really struggled in all aspects of school including with me. After having a really rough day together, I decided I needed to try something different. We discussed the learning that I had done the week before. I told this student that I learned that ALL students are genius. After a little more discussion the student grabbed a post it note and made this sign:

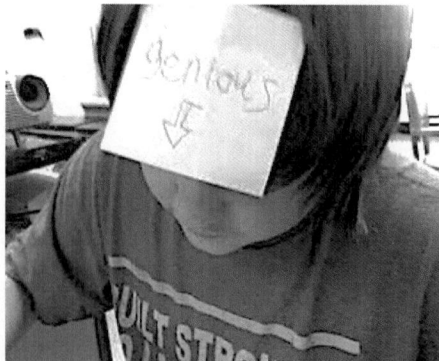

Not only did he just make the sign, but also he showed me his genius the whole period! He worked so hard and I was so proud of him. At

the end of the day he took off his sign and said, "I'll leave this here so I can save my genius for tomorrow."

All from a difference in language!"

On my blog, I regularly highlight and honor genius; students, teachers, and classrooms that are:

- Solving problems in a ways no one else could.
- Looking at the world with fresh eyes.
- Changing the rules.
- Making a unique impact on the world
- Working on becoming more compassionate, empathetic, and passionate.
- Giving the world something it didn't know was missing.

These geniuses are not only passing the test; they are changing the world.

Their stories are an important reminder and a point to take notice of in all our planning and work. As we eagerly seek to find methods, strategies, and ideas to best prepare our students for the world and work ahead; we must not forget to celebrate, cherish, and honor who they are right now, today.

Bring a video camera to class with you tomorrow. Have your digital camera on hand to capture their moments of genius - **A**lways **B**e **C**apturing - and continue to notice what they already do with grace and ease.

Children so often teach me far more than anything I could offer them. So, tomorrow, consider this in your lesson plan:

Boys and Girls,

When I watch you work, I am amazed at the genius I see. Let me give you a couple of examples... Today, I am here to let you know I have no doubt that you are capable of handling the challenging work ahead. Problems like this can only be solved by the Habitudes that you possess.

Today I need every one of them. I need your curiosity. I need your imagination. I need your willingness to persevere with me when things get tough. I need your courage, and most of all I need your passion.

We can so do this. Will you join me?

What do you think? Will genius show up? I predict that whatever skill, strategy, or standard we will work on together is no match for the geniuses that lay in wait for your acknowledgement.

The world is ready to receive their talent with arms open wide. Let's do the same.

The First 20 Days At a Glance

What are your hopes and dreams for this school year?

Many teachers ask students this question at the start of every school year. It's a conversation starter, and it sets the stage for awesome learning to follow.

While the question may seem simple, posing it to students and asking them to share their responses can have a profound effect on the classroom and community.

Just think about the messages inherent in the question: what you care about matters at school; your hopes and goals are taken seriously; you have a say in what and how we will learn.

Taking the time to help children articulate their hopes and dreams sets a tone of collaboration and mutual respect. It fosters reflection and self-knowledge by prompting children to ask themselves questions such as:

- What do I want learning to be like?
- What do I want from the experience of school?
- What matters to me most?
- What am I worried about?
- What am I most excited to learn more about and learn from?
- What am I going to become more awesome at?

Sharing hopes and dreams also creates a meaningful context for establishing classroom protocols and procedures. Once hopes have been articulated, discussions can begin about what "rules" will be needed to help everyone's hopes and dreams come true. This is the foundation and the rationale behind Genius Hour and/or Genius Time.

Genius Hour is the promise we make to one another, that our passions will matter; that we will do work that matters, and we will make time during the school day for it.

The lessons that follow are dedicated to helping students develop into better readers, writers, thinkers and most importantly passion-driven learners. To do this well in day-to-day life, students must develop patterns of thinking in which their ability is combined with their inclination to think well and their awareness of thinking opportunities. Students must have not only the opportunity to see passion- driven learning, but also to develop their own passions.

In seeking to liberate genius fully, we understand best within a classroom context in which:

1. Thinking is **valued**
2. There is **time** for thinking about our own and others passions
3. Rich **opportunities** for exploring passion
4. Passion-driven learning is regularly **modeled**
5. The process as well as the products of thinking are present in the **environment**

Such an environment sends the message that thinking is valued. In addition, it not only provides a time and place for the practice of students' skills but also provides the leverage needed to foster an inclination toward thinking and to develop a greater awareness of thinking occasions. Immersed in a classroom culture of thinking, students have the opportunity to develop patterns of behavior and thinking that become our habits.

The resources in this section are designed to help teachers collectively focus on the implicit messages about thinking being sent in classrooms and across the school.

Every successful Genius Hour will need some structure. Each day, students are told where to go and when and what to do. We need to teach them to use their independence toward a goal they create themselves, and this will take some structure. For students who initially don't cope well with a "blank sheet of paper," share a cartoon with them (http://www.gocomics.com/calvinandhobbes/1995/12/31).

As students become acclimated to this new working environment, the classroom may start to feel a bit "messy." But a bit of mess can be good when students are actively exploring their passion. They *should* be talking to their classmates about their projects, and they should be moving around the room to find the resources they need.

Passion-based Learning vs. Project-Based Learning

Genius Hour and project-based learning (PBL) were born out of a similar goal: for students to solve real-world problems in a classroom context. However, most implementations of PBL lack the single most important ingredient: passion. If students do not become giddy when they talk about their genius hour, it's just another requirement to be satisfied, wrapped up with the veneer of being innovative. This is not student-centered, and it is not the transformative learning students need for the 21st century.

Passion-based learning starts with the most essential elements of a student's humanity. It recognizes that learning is built strongly on experiences. From that foundation, a student's efforts become "real-world" to the extent that they can change the world.

Further reading/viewing:
- Passion Driven vs. Project-Drive: There is a Difference (https://www.youtube.com/watch?v=C5BFu0S4UVA)
- Let's Close the Passion Gap (http://www.angelamaiers.com/2015/02/lets-close-the-passion-gap)
- "Personal Statement" by Catherine Broyles (https://vimeo.com/86149245)

Days 1 through 7:
Accepting Your Genius

Setting Up Your Genius Notebook

Objective:

Students will learn how to record, keep and revisit their observations made during genius hour over the course of the school year.

Background:

If technology is ubiquitous in your school, then most likely you will choose a digital option for the Genius Notebook. If so, we strongly recommend OneNote, an information gathering and collaboration platform.

Visit this website, http://www.choose2matter.org/liberatinggenius/ to access a customized version of the Genius Hour notebook specifically tailored to these lessons for students.

However, also consider having students keep a separate folder or notebook to house paper photos, drawings, handwritten notes, scribbles, etc.

Other schools may rely solely on a paper notebook. If so:

- Have students bring a large bound notebook or heavy-duty three-pronged folder to class.
- Save five to ten pages at the front of the notebook to house information about it and a cumulative table of contents.
- Have them number the pages immediately so they start in an organized fashion.

Find a central location in the classroom to store the notebooks, or instruct students to bring their Genius Notebooks to class each time a lesson is taught. Encourage the students to get in the habit of reflection and reflective writing each time you meet.

Notebook Contents:

The notebook should be the student's personalized record of Genius Hour learning. The contents can include a range of materials that are relevant to the individual. The notebook should hold everything when possible.

Evaluation Suggestions:

How you assess notebook use is dependent on the ages and grade levels of your students. Don't feel compelled to formally grade the work; the purpose of the notebook is reflective in nature. Your attention to how the students use the notebook and your feedback about it as a learning tool can encourage students to use the tool consistently.

The following suggestions provide guidance for both formal and informal evaluation of the notebooks:

- Explain the purposes of the notebooks when you have the students create them.
- Explain at the outset the criteria on which the notebooks will be evaluated.
- Glance at the notebooks each day for the first few weeks of the semester.
- Walk around and give positive comments as students are using their notebooks.
- Use a symbol to monitor timely accomplishment of assignments.
- Build use of the notebooks into the Genius Hour lessons.
- Schedule small-group sessions for students who need extra support in using the notebook effectively.
- Model and support note taking as appropriate for your students' ages and grade levels.
- Don't feel compelled to grade every notebook entry or collect a few each day over a period of time.

- Require students to do a self-assessment of their notebooks.

Introducing the Notebook:

An example of the narrative I use to introduce the notebook follows.

This interactive notebook is more than a place to take notes. It is a way of collecting and processing information. Great scholars, artists, and scientists have used notebooks like these and found them to be powerful tools to increase their knowledge, productivity, and expertise. This method of reflective thinking and learning can serve you as well.

- *Think about your thinking*
- *Apply what you are learning to your own studies*
- *Become better question-askers*
- *Tap into your creative side*
- *Remain open to continuous learning*

I'm sure you could think of many other benefits! This is your notebook. You are going to keep it for yourself. There is not one right way to record your thoughts and plans. It helps you process and record the important points from our conversations. More importantly, it will help you reflect on what you wish to do with that information and how you might apply the lessons in your study and life.

This week, we will practice exploring a few tools and templates that you may want to include in your notebook. I have some examples if you would like to see how other learners have organized theirs. It is important you find something that works for you. Your notebook will be the key to your success in these lessons. At the end of the year, you will have your notes, handouts, and valuable information concerning the habitudes all in one place. I am excited to get our notebooks organized and ready to go!

Discussion Questions for Setting Up Your Genius Notebook:

- What went well with the setup?
- What was challenging? How did you overcome it?
- What adjustments did you make for your class?
- If you were to do it again, what would you do differently?

Introduction to Genius Hour

"Don't ask yourself what the world needs, ask yourself what makes you come alive. And then go and do THAT.

Because what the world needs is people who have come alive."

HOWARD THURMAN
AUTHOR + PHILOSOPHER

Objective:

Students will understand what Genius Hour is and why it is important.

Background:

What makes genius hour different is the focus on the process of students becoming more engaged in their work.

One of the best things students will get to do in our Genius Hour is pick their own topics and areas of passion to explore. Students may explore these topics alone or with other students sharing their same passion.

But, that is not the only thing they will be doing.

As we think back on how our classrooms are run, the things geniuses need are sometimes left out. Recognizing genius in our students is more than an act of encouragement or a well-meaning attempt to boost self-esteem; it is critical in our efforts in preparing our students for the global environment that thrives on critical thinking, problem solving, collaboration, innovation and effective communication. It's our job to nurture our geniuses so they can change the world.

In a speech given at the 2009 Annual Meeting of National Academy of Sciences, President Barack Obama, brought the importance of passion to the front and center of the academic debate:

"The call and need of a new era is for greatness. It's for fulfillment, passionate execution and significant contribution. We know students can rise up to the challenge and do amazing work. They can do genius work!"

To ensure "No genius is left behind," we must consider and commit to a culture and curriculum that honors, nurtures, and sustains the genius in every individual. We must nurture a culture that requires and expects students to demonstrate their genius, and empowers them to share their personal genius with the world.

Lesson #1:

Introduction (~ 20 minutes)

We're going to do something brand new in our classroom.

To get our brains ready, we're going to think critically about this quote:

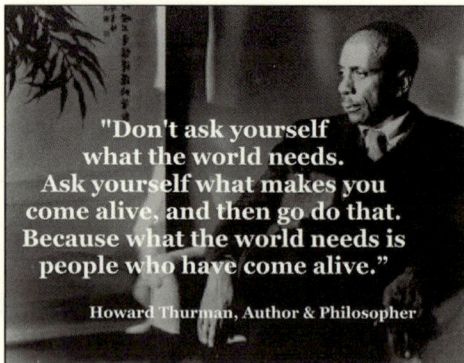

"Don't ask yourself what the world needs. Ask yourself what makes you come alive, and then go do that. Because what the world needs is people who have come alive."

Howard Thurman, Author & Philosopher

Ask students to sit with these ideas for a minute.

Discussion:

- *What does it mean to come alive?*
- *What are some things that make people come alive?*
- *What are some reasons it might be important to come alive/share our passions with the world?*
- *Why does the world need people to come alive?*

What does this quote have to do with the new part of our class? Well, the new part of our class is called Genius Hour, and it's all about coming alive.

Most of the time that you are in school, teachers decide what you will study. But during Genius Hour, you get to decide what you learn about and how you spend your time. Many of the lessons we study will help you discover whatever it is that makes you come alive.

We will have Genius Hour [specify the frequency and duration, i.e. every day for 45 minutes, or every Tuesday morning for one hour, etc. - whatever fits in your classroom schedule).

This is something that classrooms all around the world, have been doing for a couple of years. I can't wait to embark on this journey with you all.

Throughout our time of doing Genius Hour, we will be keeping a Genius notebook. We'll talk in more detail about this Genius notebook later on, but to start, we're going to journal some of our initial thoughts about Genius Hour.

- *What are my thoughts on Genius Hour?*
- *What are my questions about Genius Hour?*
- *What am I excited about?*
- *What am I nervous about?*

(These initial journal entries can help you to assess where your students may need some more guidance, and which students may struggle at first with their own plans. Also, ask students to share their journal entries with their parents, to encourage family support for the students' efforts and explorations in Genius Hour.)

Discussion Questions for Introduction to Genius Hour:

- How did you learn about genius hour and what were your first impressions coming into this study?
- What are your initial questions about Genius Hour?
- What about Genius Hour excites you?
- What about Genius Hour makes you nervous?

What Is Genius?

Objective:

Students will understand the definition of a genius, and that we all have genius capacity

Background:

Many people think of genius the way that the Merriam Webster dictionary defines it:

ge·nius (noun)

1: extraordinary intellectual power especially as manifested in creative activity

2: a person endowed with transcendent mental superiority; specifically: a person with a very high IQ

But does this definition encompass the full spectrum of genius? Do LeBron James and Taylor Swift have "extraordinary intellectual power"? Many people believe that genius is more about the uniquely inspired output of a process, rather than a static personality trait or the meaning we assign to a score on an IQ test.

Genius is developed talent applied in a new or novel way. In other words, we believe genius is less a function of nature than it is a matter of nurture. It isn't something reserved for a special few. It's something accessible to each of us.

Like many, I grew up believing that only a special gifted few could become extraordinary. Too often, genius is presented as a rare gift—something in one's DNA, rather than attributes that could be learned throughout one's life.

In fact, this problem is centuries old—even Einstein and Edison were not recognized for the gifts they possessed. Imagine what they might have achieved with such self-knowledge! Our students deserve to be told early and often that they, too, were born with the potential for genius.

You may not know whether the future Marie Curie or the next Shakespeare is sitting in your classroom. What can be confirmed is this: learners who believe they have unique abilities early on will be more likely than others to…

- Harness their talents more quickly
- Develop self-confidence and a belief that they can succeed
- Maintain their optimism and confidence under stress
- Learn to rely on themselves more than others to get what they need in life
- Live a productive and fulfilled life

The world has been changed by ordinary individuals who were blessed enough to have been encouraged and empowered to become extraordinary.

Once you understand and believe that you are capable of the extraordinary, you will not settle for the ordinary.

The same observation applies to your students. Once you have nurtured them in the habitudes, they will realize the strength of their capabilities to be imaginative, curious, self-aware, persistent, courageous, passionate and adaptable. For this development to occur, we must understand and communicate four principles through our instruction.

Materials:

Below are three books and three videos that could supplement this lesson. In our written lesson, we only include one of the videos, but you might decide to use more than one and one or more of the books as well.

Books:

Your Fantastic Elastic Brain by JoAnn Deak - This book shows children that they have the capability to stretch and grow their brains. It also shows the anatomy of the brain.

I Can be Anything by Jerry Spinelli - This book takes readers through hopes and dreams while showing them life's possibilities are endless!

Dot by Peter Reynolds - Vashti thinks she cannot draw. Her teacher tells her to "make a mark and see where it takes you." Vashti merely draws a dot on her paper, and her teacher then says, "Now sign it." The next week Vashti is surprised to see her dot framed on display in the teacher's office. She says, "I can make a better dot than that." She then starts drawing elaborate, colorful dots and realizes she is indeed an artist.

Videos:

Lion Lights: Having found his family's only bull dead after an attack from lions, Richard Turere, a 13-year-old from the Masai community in Kenya, felt there had to be a way to protect his family's livestock from the lions who roam over from Nairobi National Park. Yet he wanted to do so without killing or harming the lions, as many of his tribesmen did.

(https://www.ted.com/talks/richard_turere_a_peace_treaty_with_the_l ions)

After scarecrows failed to work, Richard took to walking around his cowshed with a torch. He realized that lions were afraid of moving light. Using parts from a broken flashlight and a motorcycle, he created solar powered flashing lights that kept the lions away from his family's cowshed. His invention has now been adopted at farms all over Kenya. His invention earned him the chance to speak at the TED conference and a scholarship to Brookhouse International School in Kenya.

Here's to the Crazy Ones: Genius hour challenges students to break the mold on what school is supposed to be. It demands that they "Think Different" - the mantra of Apple, which produced this one-minute commercial in 1997. A montage of video of some of the finest revolutionaries of the 20th century is overlaid with the voice of actor Richard Dreyfus, saying, "They change things. They push the human race forward. While some see them as the crazy ones, we see genius. Because the ones crazy enough to think they can change the world, are the ones who do."

(https://www.youtube.com/watch?v=D9T_5MeFA1M)

Caine's Arcade: 9-year-old Caine Monroy spent his summer vacation building an elaborate cardboard arcade inside his dad's used auto parts store. On the last day of summer, a filmmaker named Nirvan became Caine's first customer. Watch Caine's Arcade to see what happened next - and how Caine reacted to it!

(https://vimeo.com/40000072)

Lesson:

So, what is a genius?

Part 1: (~20 minutes)

Have you heard the word genius? What does it mean to you? (Write and share student responses)

A brilliant writer named Mr. Seth Godin writes that genius is the act of solving a problem in a way no one has solved it before.

He says genius is not someone who was born smart or can do really hard math problems or memorize a lot of things. He says genius is the act of finding original solutions that matter. A genius looks at something that others are stuck on and gets the world unstuck.

We're going to watch this video by a 13 year-old boy from Kenya named Richard. Let's note what was the problem that Richard wanted to solve, and how he did it, and the steps he had to take to find his solution.

(Chart student responses)
Anyone and everyone can demonstrate genius. But as we saw in this video with Richard, genius takes time, effort and hard work, and usually you have to try a lot of solutions that don't work before you find one that does. Are you willing to do that work? I know you can do it and I'm here to help.

Part 2: (~20 minutes)

Let's brainstorm some problems in our lives that we think we might want to solve. (Chart on board).

Let's get to work on practicing our genius. I'd like for all of us to use our genius together to think about how we could solve a problem here at school. (Choose one that relates to school).

Let's try to answer these questions about the problem we chose:

14

- *How can we make it better?*
- *Is this what is needed most?*
- *What is it we hope to accomplish and what's stopping us?*
- *What are we most proud of?*
- *What is possible?*
- *When can we start?*
- *How will we prevent failure?*
- *Who/how can we make this happen?*
- *What do we regret most?*
- *How can we make the best use of...?*
- *What if we...(Dream big!)*

Which ones relate to our problem? (Star those that students choose).

Let's try to answer these. (Solicit student answers).

Now, I want you to practice your genius work on your own. You can choose a new problem that speaks to you or continue working on the one we did together. Now, I want you to look at these questions and think about the problem you are trying to solve. Not all of the questions will relate to your problem. Read through them and choose one or two questions to start with.

Write your problem and question(s) on your paper. Take some time to really think about what you're going to do to help with this problem. I will set the timer for 10 minutes. I will walk around and talk with you. You may not finish, but being a genius takes time and hard work. Use your brain. Think things through. It may get messy. But that's what being a genius is all about.

Phrases to use with students:

- *What are you thinking about?*
- *What made you think about this? Tell me more.*
- *Why is this so important?*
- *What research will you need to do?*

Discussions Questions for What Is Genius:

- In your own words, how do you define the word **genius**?
- How did brainstorming about different ways of problem solving help you define the term, **genius**?
- How did the series of questions accelerate your discussion and support your ability to problem solve?
- Reflect on your student's journey; how has their definition of **genius** evolved from the beginning of the lesson to the end?

How Do Genius Learners Work?

Objective:

Create the mindset of being a Genius Learner to prepare students to explore and share their genius

Background:

Genius is misunderstood as a bolt of lightning. -Seth Godin, Author

You can't settle for the ordinary when you comprehend you're extraordinary. I hope this statement echoes in your mind as you learn about Genius Hour and use this book with your students.

A careful study of science, history, philosophy and theology emerges a discernable pattern followed by every successful citizen leader. Namely, anyone and everyone who has added significant value to the world around them did so by establishing a cycle of virtuous change by willfully *illuminating, cultivating, replicating and celebrating* the unique potential and genius in those around them.

In other words, they liberated themselves from catering to the court of public opinion and committed to fighting for a cause they believed in. They are clear eyed on who they are and what they stand for, unafraid to amplify their best and work on those areas where they can grow, and choose to march boldly forward in the direction of their dreams.

Genius isn't a label reserved for the chosen few—the poets, painters, sculptors, scientists, or writers—it's an opportunity to become the best possible version of ourselves at a time when the world needs our unique, special and stand-alone contribution. Today, perhaps more than ever.

Lesson:

Conduct a jigsaw activity for students to learn about successful people and what helped them to achieve that success and share their gifts with the world.

For information on how to conduct a jigsaw:
http://www.readwritethink.org/professional-development/strategy-guides/using-jigsaw-cooperative-learning-30599.html

Some of our favorite historical examples of people who exemplify sharing their genius with the world include Marie Curie, Albert Einstein, Thomas Edison, Amelia Earhart, Elizabeth Blackwell, Michelangelo, and Leonardo Da Vinci. People currently popular with students who arguably qualify as genius learners include Taylor Swift, Steve Jobs, Sheryl Sandberg, Derek Jeter, Peyton Manning, and Meryl Streep.

Here is a series of 1,000+ biographies, indexed by profession, genders, and race or region of origin; it includes many of the people who we've listed (http://www.sweetsearch.com/biographies).

After students have completed the jigsaw, have students work with their jigsaw group, and then as a whole class, to compile a list of attributes and habits that they noticed in these successful people.

Talk about how these people were not just born with an extraordinary talent and immediately successful, they worked hard and had to practice sharing it with the world. Just like these role models, we each have a genius and Genius Hour is just the beginning of sharing it with the world. Consider sharing this video of Michael Jordan, and asking them to reflect on it.

https://www.youtube.com/watch?v=PH8nTfxwByY

This is a meaningful time to share the Genius Hour mantra with your students, and display it in your classroom.

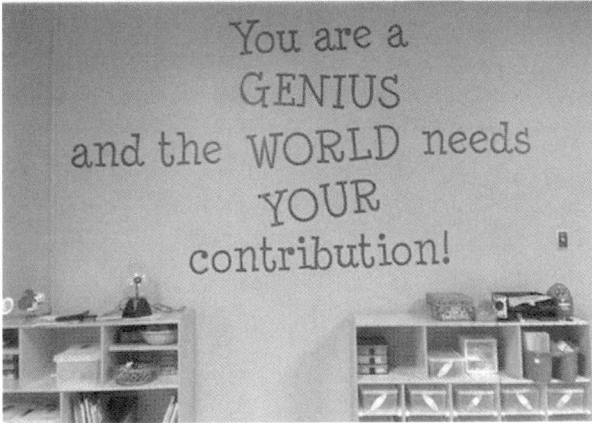

Ultimately learning "how geniuses think" is about problem solving, creativity and the creation of excellence. We hope that by sharing strategies of genius, students will develop the tools they need to contribute to the world and help solve some of its biggest problems.

For example, by modeling the innovation strategies of genius inventors, our hope is that our students may one day devise solutions to minimize pollution and make our planet healthier. Or, by modeling how genius teachers inspire their students, a whole new wave of teachers will engage students in a way that will ignite the love of learning and passion to create new things in the world. The chance to change the world is what drives us.

Through our involved deconstruction process, we've learned that being a genius is not about raw talent, bigger brains, or superior genetics. It's about highly effective and exceptionally streamlined mental strategies. With the right mental strategies in place, anyone can achieve "genius" results.

Discussions Questions for How Do Genius Learners Work:

- What are your initial thoughts about how to create the mindset of a Genius Leader and prepare students to explore and share their genius?
- The jigsaw activity is one approach to expose students to the attributes, strengths and habits of successful people; what are some other ways you could analyze these genius leaders?
- How does this deconstructive process help students learn about what it means to be a genius?
- What was one thing that surprised you when learning about the geniuses? Why did it surprise you?

What is My Genius?

"**You** ARE A **GENIUS** AND THE **WORLD** NEEDS YOUR **CONTRIBUTION.**"
→ ANGELA MAIERS

Background:

When introducing Genius hour, it can be daunting for students to choose their own passion to explore, as many students have never been asked this before. To build the foundation for Genius Hour, students must first gain self-awareness of their own genius.

Before you begin preparing for this unit, read "Nurturing Student Genius." It contains some stellar responses from students when asked the question "What is your genius?" The comments from my community are also very insightful.

http://www.angelamaiers.com/2011/01/nurturing-genius

Lesson: What is my Genius?

Part 1: What makes me, me? (~10 minutes)

Introduce this question: what makes me, me?

Have students select one or more of the following questions to respond to in their Genius Hour Notebook:

- What makes me to smile, laugh, or get excited?
- What catches my attention or keeps me interest?
- What do I always manage to find the time to do?

- What do I think about most - even when I don't have time for it?
- What are some interesting things I have done/seen in my life?
- What do I know a lot about?
- What words do others use to describe me?
- What words do I use to describe myself?
- When I am alone, I almost always . . .
- When I am with my friends, we most like to . . .
- How am I different than my friends?
- What makes me unique?
- What makes me most happy?
- What do I most love to do?

Now use your answers to help you answer this question: What makes me, me?

Students can respond in any way to these prompts—writing, illustrating, or reflecting. The goal is self-awareness and expression. There are no right or wrong answers—only discoveries.

Part 2: What do my classmates see in me? (~10 minutes)

Some students may struggle pinpointing their own genius, and others will overlook things that their classmates may notice about them.

For this part of the activity, each student will write their name on the top of a piece of paper, and tape it to their back. Then, all of the students walk around the room, and anonymously write what they think their classmates' genius is on that student's paper.

When the activity is over, each student will have an additional list of what their classmates think they are good at/what they notice about them. This not only helps students who may struggle with self-awareness, but also can be affirming for students who may have lower self-esteem. Teachers are encouraged to join in the activity for this part.

At the end of the activity, students will have 2 sources of inspiration of their genius. In their Genius Notebooks, have students reflect:

- Did your classmates notice genius in you that you did not have notice yourself?
- Did you learn anything new about yourself?

Encourage students to continue brainstorming their genius to help them begin to build the foundation of their own genius hour focus.

Supplemental Lesson: My One Special Thing!

For students ready to work at a more advanced level, consider substituting the following lesson instead, or adding it to the above lesson.

In this lesson, I have students work with partners to explore further what makes individuals unique. This lesson expands on the approach used in the prior, in which students were determining how to answer the question, what makes me, me? The conversation with students and the activity I have them complete follows.

Putting into words who we are and what makes us special is sometimes hard to do. It is important to find friends and mentors who will help us in the process of self-discovery. Today, we are going to work with partners helping one another reflect on the unique and special aspects of our lives and stories.

The questions your partner will be asking you are intended to help you discover the things that make you stand out and special. Knowing your talents, passions, and gifts will help you know what to work on as a learner and friend, but also will help you work as a more productive community citizen because you will know exactly what you have to contribute to the world.

Remember, some of our best talents are hidden. Let your partner help you uncover exactly what those talents are.

The following questions can be used to guide and focus the students' interviews with each other. I discuss each question with the students using the examples to help them broaden their thinking about themselves as they interview one another. Comments and examples I discuss with the students accompany each question.

1. Your knowledge: What do you know a lot about?

Your knowledge may be about anything and can come from any source. It could be about animals, sports, musical instruments, history, building or creating something, surviving a difficult time, handling a sickness or disease, secrets to being healthy or happy, or making others happy.

2. Your skills: What do you know how to do well?

These may include skills developed and used at school, around the house, in sports or games, with hobbies, in recreational activities, or in anything else that you do. Examples: training, experiments, competing or being a competitor, reading well, studying, new technology, video games, taking care of someone, or something else.

3. Your strengths: What is the characteristic that you are most known for?

When people describe you, what do they say you are good at? Examples: I'm very disciplined. I'm always positive and happy. I always make people feel good or happy. I'm careful. I can really be trusted. I'm not afraid to say what I am thinking.

4. Your abilities: What kinds of things do you believe you have a talent for?

Examples: I have the ability to organize things. I have the ability to get my friends and family motivated. I'm good at fixing things.

5. Your interests: What kinds of things do you *love* to do?

Examples: What have you dreamed of doing if you had the chance to actually do it? What have you not tried but would like to? What do you like to do in your free time?

6. Your experience: What are some interesting things you have done and seen in your life?

Our personal experiences not only shape what we know, they can shape who we are and may become. Even if the experiences we have may be ones that we do not wish to repeat, every experience is an important learning tool. Think about what you have experienced that could be used to help you in this new project. What experiences were the most exciting? Difficult? Remarkable? What have you done that you might want build on?

Examples: I traveled to another country. I have met someone who . . . I played the piano for five years. I was a part of a club. I tried something scary and I learned to . . . I volunteered.

7. Your one special thing!

This interview was a treasure map leading us to uncover all your hidden talents. What is the one special thing that stands out now?

Discussions Questions for What Is My Genius:

- How did you introduce this pivotal lesson with your students? What went well? What would you have changed and why?
- Reflect on your students' reactions to their peers recognizing their genius. How do you think this activity helped students see their own genius?
- How did the interview questions elicit your students to respond about themselves? Were there any 'eye-opening' comments or answers?

Proud to Be Me

Objective:

Identify the importance of "owning your own genius" using a book or personal story.

Background:

One of my favorite stories about uniqueness is *Only One You* by Linda Kranz.

It is a powerful story of letting one's genius shine, even if it is different from the norm. It is a wonderful opportunity to discuss with students the balance of "blending in and standing out" we need to find when we are finding our own way.

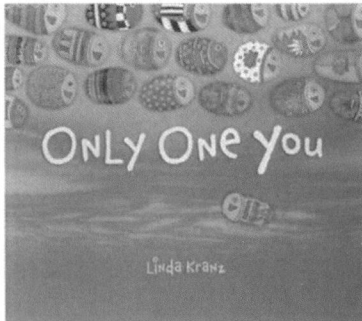

From the publisher:

"There's only one you in this great big world. Make it a better place. Adri's mama and papa share some of the wisdom they have gained through the years with their eager son. Their words, simple and powerful, are meant to comfort and guide him as he goes about exploring the world. This exquisitely illustrated book explodes with color and honest insights. Kranz's uniquely painted rockfish, set against vibrant blue seas, make an unforgettable and truly special impression. *Only One You* will inspire parents and children of all ages as they swim through life."

Materials Needed:

Only One You (or another book with a similar theme; *Stellaluna, The Ugly Duckling* and *Amazing Grace* are but a few); Chart paper

Lesson:

This is a story about what it means to be unique. (Feel free to let students share their ideas on what it means to be unique.)

Then, read *Only One You* by Linda Kranz (or alternative book).

Lesson Activity: (~20 minutes)

After reading the story, discuss with students:

1. *What makes a person stand out from other people?*
2. *How can people stand out in a good way in the classroom? In the cafeteria? On the playground? At home?*

Discuss how it might feel to perform standout behavior. Do you feel pride? Happiness? Satisfaction?

Using a large piece of butcher paper, create a heading: "Stand Out Behavior! We Sparkle and Shine."

Continue brainstorming ways people can stand out in a good way, and list them on the chart. Use the chart as a reference for modeling and encouraging standout behavior in the classroom, such as:

- Taking turns
- Holding the door for others
- Listening politely when someone is speaking
- Following directions
- Helping others
- Sharing smiles with one another

Adri's parents also share that you don't have to follow the crowd. Use this wisdom to discuss:

- *What does it mean to follow the crowd?*
- *When might it not be a good idea to follow the crowd?*
(When the crowd is making bad choices or misbehaving, etc.)

Ask students to share instances of when they've made their own choices, without following the crowd.

Discussions Questions for Proud to Be Me:
- What do you think makes a person stand out from other people?
- How will you or how do you, encourage students to stand out in a positive way? Why do you think this works?
- How does it feel to stand out and perform well? How do you think your students feel when they do the same? Pride? Happiness? Satisfaction?
- How can you encourage your students to complement one another and notice good behavior?
- How do you think the book, *Only One You* by Linda Kranz helped your students understand when it might not be a good idea to follow the crowd?
- How do you encourage students to make their own choices and be independent? Why do you think this is important?

What Do I Want to Be?

Objective:

Students will understand the difference between *doing* and *being*—between actions and inner transformation—and how the two affect each other. Students will relate this concept to their own unique genius.

Background:

In our task-oriented work world, it is tempting to feel under the thumb of the to-do list. Having tangible items helps us stay organized, but that focus has a downside: it pulls our attention into the micro-world of projects, planning, and deadlines. Students deserve a different focus.

Our success is attributed not only to what we do; it is dependent on who we are. We set young leaders up to fall if we encourage them to envision what they can do before first considering the kind of kind of student and leader they want to be. If we focus on what it's important *to be*, knowing what *to do* becomes much easier.

What students *do* and what they want to *be* should be tightly linked. In this lesson, we turn our attention to getting students *to be* successful learners and leaders. In addition, we show them what that looks like—the actions that lead to that transformation.

In today's lesson, students will reflect on the person they hope to be, and they will see that choosing actions are the way to make that change a reality.

To see one example of this in action, read "A To BE List for Aspiring Leaders." After students complete this lesson, share this piece with them (or an abridged form, for younger students), in order to reinforce these ideas.

http://switchandshift.com/a-to-be-list-for-aspiring-leaders-by-angela-maiers

Materials:

Have the students create a "worksheet" in their Genius Hour notebook as follows:

Being and Doing
I want to become . . .
These actions are my "bricks" . . . (1) (2) (3)
How do my actions look? (1) (2) (3)
My genius is . . .
One action for this is . . .
The way that I do it is . .

Lesson:

Part 1: (~20 minutes)

Theme: WHAT you are doing/being

Display the following quote and read it out loud:

"We form habits, and then they form us."
– Dr. Rob Gilbert, Professor of Sports Psychology

What does this quote mean to you? (Discuss with students for 1-5 minutes).

Many of you have an idea of what kind of person you want to be. You might want to be a good student who gets high grades, or a good friend, or a good sibling to you brother or sister. Today, we are going to learn how to become that person.

Now, in order to accomplish something, we need to make a goal. So, we need to first make sure that you have a clear picture of that person you want to become.

Take a few minutes now and think about the person you'd like to become. You might use adjectives like courageous, friendly, helpful, and hard working. You might also think of roles that you have, like your role as a student or sibling we mentioned before. Don't limit yourself to the kind of things I've said. Think really hard about whom you want to be. After you've given it a lot of thought, write down in your Genius Notebook all of the ideas that come to mind.

(Allow about 5 minutes for students to work).

Let's share some of the excellent ideas you came up with.

Ask students to share their ideas as a class. Affirm and acknowledge the quality of their contributions, and when possible connect their answers to what you have noticed in them. E.g. *"I can tell that you are concerned about being a good friend by the way you treat your fellow students."*

Now that we know what we'd like to be, the next step is knowing what to do. Imagine that who you want to be is a building made up of small but sturdy bricks. Each brick is an action. Every time you act, you add a brick to who you want to be. Over time, those bricks create something big and long lasting.

(In this next part, use an example from another student to complete the explanation).

For example, Kristen said that she wants to be more helpful. If she is chooses to help clear the dishes after dinner, what kind of brick goes into her building? (Ask students for their responses). *What if she chooses to leave the table without helping? What kind of brick is that?* (Ask students for their responses).

Now look at the things you have listed. Start with three of your favorite items on your list. What are the actions that would be good bricks? Write down as many ideas as you can for those three items.

Allow students about 5 minutes to write their responses.

Let's share a few of your ideas. (Ask students for their response.)

Optional: Have one or two students act out one of their responses.

Part 2: (~20 minutes)

Theme: HOW you're doing/being it

Explain how doing something good isn't necessarily "being" something good.

e.g. Visiting a friend but being in a bad mood
e.g. Schoolwork that you don't necessarily like: do you huff and puff about it? Or do you get it done because you know it's your responsibility?

32

Now each of you has a list of actions that will be like bricks to build the building of who you want to be. But, there is a secret to making those bricks strong and not just look like they're strong. Let me give you an example.

If I want to be a good friend, choosing to go hang out with a friend who is having a bad day is a good decision, right? Now, what if I showed up to my friend's house and acted this:

(In a bored, disengaged manner) *Hey, how's it going . . . Ok, whatever, that's cool . . .* (Pretend to take out cell phone and be more interested in it than conversation) *Hey, do you have anything to eat?*

What is wrong with that? (Ask for student responses.)

Exactly. That's because it's not just <u>what</u> *you do. It's* <u>how</u> *you do it. You need to remember those ideas of who you want to be and make sure that your actions match it. Let's try another example. If I wanted to be a good student, how would I act when it came time to do my homework? How would I* <u>not</u> *act?*

(Ask for student responses).

Take a look at the actions you have written down, the "bricks" that make up who you want to be. Use the next few minutes to write down <u>how</u> *you would make those decisions and you how you might* <u>not</u> *make those decisions.*

(Allow about 5 minutes for student work. Share responses as a class).

These are some amazing ideas you are all sharing! Finally, I want you to remember your genius from a few days ago. (Day 5: What is My Genius?) *Does everybody remember? Take a few moments and think about* <u>how</u> *your genius acts. I'll give you one minute.*
After one minute, give them an example of how to declare their genius, and then add a way that genius would interact.

Here is an example. My genius is being incredibly patient. One action for being patient is to get into line when there is a wait for something. The way that I do this is to not get frustrated, roll my eyes, and complain about having to wait.

Write the following three things:

- *What your genius is.*
- *An action that demonstrates your genius.*
- *How you do that action to make sure it matches your genius.*

Discussions Questions for What Do I Want to Be?

- How do you think our actions affect who we are?
- How do you think the "bricks" in your life influence decision making?
- Why is it important to emphasize the kind of student and leader they want to **be** first? How will knowing what **to do** therefore be easier to determine afterwards? Can you think of concrete examples that prove that actions lead to transformation?

Days 8 through 13: Accelerating Your Genius

My Passion, My Heart

Objective:

Students will learn how to create "heart maps" to begin to identify what matters most to them.

Background:

The stories we tell not only give others information about our lives—who we are, what we do, and why we do it—but also enable us to reflect on our behaviors and what they mean. It is important to give students the opportunity to discover themselves by exploring their personal story.

The best stories come straight from the heart. My favorite strategy for helping students find the way to their hearts and tell their story is called heart mapping, based on the book, *Awakening the Heart* by Georgia Heard.

Lesson:

Here is an example of the conversation I have with students:

One of the best ways we can get to know one another is through our story. Great writers and storytellers speak from their hearts. In order to do that, we have to do some work first to know what's in our *hearts, to know what we really care about, and what's really important about our lives that we want to share with others. Georgia Heard is a writer who describes getting to know your heart in her book <u>Awakening the Heart</u>.*

We are going to use a technique that Heard calls heart mapping. It is one that poets, writers, storytellers, and leaders use. Your heart map is a representation of all the important things that are in your heart, all the things that matter to you. The map can include anything that has stayed in your heart because you care a lot about it—people and places you care about, moments and memories that have stayed with you, or things you love to do.

Let's think about some questions to get us started on creating our heart maps:

- *What has really affected your heart?*
- *What people have been important to you?*
- *What are some experiences or central events that you will never forget?*
- *What happy or sad memories do you have?*
- *What secrets have you kept in your heart?*
- *What small or big things are important to you?*

As students display and share whom they are and what they are most passionate about, I use these additional questions to help them explore the ideas further and take the conversation even deeper:

- *Should some things be outside the heart and others inside?*
- *Do you want to draw more than one heart? Happy or sad? Secret or open?*
- *What's at the center of your heart? What occupies the outer edges?*
- *Do different colors represent different emotions, events, or relationships?*
- *Are there parts of your heart you are willing to share with others? Parts you want to keep private- how will you represent both?*

How we see ourselves inside determines how and why we do our work with and around others. It is the work of knowing ourselves from the inside out that allows us to work successfully on the outside. Heart maps are a wonderful way to sharpen that inner vision.

- The students' participation in this activity may vary. Sometimes I'll record students' contributions on chart paper or a whiteboard.

- Other times, I let the conversation flow without providing any written support.

- Alternatively, I sometimes conclude the lesson by having students record their heart maps in their Genius Notebooks.

- I encourage them to review their heart maps periodically to add new ideas that show their growth in self-awareness.

For other examples of heart-mapping activities with students, with vivid images of the completed process, read:

Ruth Manna's post on Scholastic:
http://blogs.scholastic.com/top_teaching/2011/01/heart-maps-and-writing.html

Helping Students Choose2Matter, by Karen McMillan:
http://www.notesfrommcteach.com/2013/06/helping-students-choose2matter-part-2.html

Heartbreak Mapping in Actions by Joy Kirr:
http://www.angelamaiers.com/2013/11/heartbreak-mapping-in-action/

Discussions Questions for My Passion, My Heart:

- How does digging deep into your heartbreak influence our actions and behavior?
- Reflect on how this lesson impacted your students. Did you learn something new about your students? How did this lesson propel their reflection?
- How does personal storytelling affect your students? Do you notice anything different when students experienced the heartbreak mapping?
- How did you share your students' heartbreak maps? What went well? What would you have done differently and why?

My Passion Profile

Objective:

I recently discovered a tool that can help provide more of a framework for helping kids to discover and pursue a passion.

Background:

Thrively is a website for students, teachers and parents that combines strength-based learning principles with amazing real world experiences. It's a terrific way to start when launching Genius Hour in the classroom. It not only can help students discover a new passion, but also pursue that passion once they've found it.

Sign up at www.thrively.com/classroom or send questions to info@thrively.com.

Discover Strengths:

Begin with Thrively's Strength Assessment. Two pediatric experts in California who specialize in childhood development created this "soft skills" survey. This is the perfect exercise to do at the beginning of the year, or when you start Genius Hour, so you can get to know your students a little better and help them get to know themselves a little better, too.

The online quiz takes about 30 minutes and can be done in one class period. The questions examine 23 different strength areas, such as focus, compassion, leadership, analytical ability, and more. The result of the quiz is a personal Strength Profile that is uplifting, positive, and energizing.

Your students will see once they finish the Strength Assessment a positive write-up showing their top 5 strengths, what they mean, and how they can apply them in life.

After your students have taken the Strength Assessment and reviewed the results, ask them to take ten minutes to reflect in their Genius Notebook on whether they agree with the findings, and how they feel about them.

Discussions Questions for My Passion Profile:

- How do you think a Strength Assessment helps your students? Were there any surprises that stood out?
- How did your students feel about their results?
- How do you see your students using the results to propel their genius?
- Now that you know your students' strengths, how can you support them so they capitalize on this insight?

My Passion Practice

Background:

Once students have taken the Strength Assessment, they can then learn how to build upon the strengths and their interests. Today's lesson will revolve around exploring these aspects of Thrively.

Explore Enrichment:

Thrively matches strengths found during the assessment to an enormous variety of real-world opportunities, such as camps, apps, internships, and even field trips. These resources have been "crowdsourced" by people from all over the world.

It can recommend an educational app to the whole class to support what they are learning in school, volunteer opportunities to help them complete required service hours, or a camp to a student with a passion for a certain interest.

Learn About Career Pathways:

Students can explore interesting career pathways and what it takes to pursue them. View day-in-the-life videos of real professionals at work. Explore activity offerings in your area that could give students a taste of what that career could be like.

Track Experiences:

Students can add activities to their profile that they have done in the past, to help build the foundation for a Digital Portfolio. When students track their "highlights," they'll be able to reference them easily in the future when it comes time for college or internship applications.

Ignite a Spark:

The Sparks section of Thrively is a collection of websites that contain enrichment designed for students. The content is embedded into the Thrively site, so students get the benefit of carefully curated news and enrichment while never leaving Thrively. Read current events, learn how to code, do creative writing exercises, view suggested reading lists, learn about music history, and more. Students can write journal entries about what they've read or learned, which you can read right from your teacher dashboard.

Snapshot:

Teachers and Principals get to see a "snapshot" of the strengths, interests, and career aspirations at the heart of your student body.

While Genius Hour will reveal your students' passions, turning them into concrete activities can be game-changing; tools like Thrively are crucial in getting students to make the leap outside the classroom walls.

Discussions Questions for My Passion Practice:

- After looking at Thrively and encouraging students to match their strengths during the assessment to real-world opportunities, how are you supporting and fostering your students in this stage?
- Have any of your students unleashed an inner passion? Share your success stories.
- How can you engage students who are holding back and refraining from engaging?

- What have your students done to change their passions into concrete activities or actions both inside and outside the classroom walls?

The World Needs Your Contribution – NOW

Objective:

Students will learn that they are ready and able to change the world - today!

Background:

A few summers ago, a student wrote a blog post about a group service trip to a third-world country. He described very challenging living conditions. He reported that the whole group vowed "to come back here and help one day." He concluded his post by vowing again to return "when I grow up."

What is he waiting for?

People of every age can begin to change the world today. Right now. This very second.

Show students that you take their ideas seriously and believe there is a global audience for those ideas. In time, students will believe the same.

Some educators and parents actually tell us that we shouldn't tell students they are geniuses who can change the world, because it sets unrealistic expectations.

Unrealistic for whom?

Fortunately, we've seen again and again how little it takes to bring this genius back to the surface and set students on their path to changing the world.

What happens when students decide they can change the world?

They do.

Lesson:

As is always the case, adults today are talking about our young people and trying to define who the students of this generation are.

One view was expressed in an article by Joel Klein in Time Magazine, titled "Millennials: The Me Me Me Generation."

http://time.com/247/millennials-the-me-me-me-generation/

Depending on their age, have students read this article, or read it to them (in whole or in part).

Ask them to react to the article. Do they think it fairly describes their generation? Does it fairly describe them? Is this who they want to be, and how they want their generation to be known?

I have quite another view of students today, as expressed in this article: http://switchandshift.com/an-open-letter-to-millennials-thank-you-for-what-i-see-in-you.

Again, depending on their age, have students read this article, or read it to them (in whole or in part).

Ask them to react to the article. Do they think it fairly describes their generation? Does it fairly describe them? Is this who they want to be, and how they want their generation to be known?

Advanced students may want to also read, "A Beginner's Mind," and ponder the following quote:

http://www.fastcompany.com/918964/beginners-mind

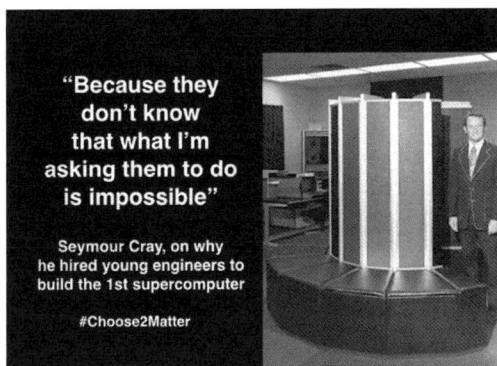

"Because they don't know that what I'm asking them to do is impossible"

Seymour Cray, on why he hired young engineers to build the 1st supercomputer

#Choose2Matter

Now let's consider the stories of a few young people who recently have changed the world. Read several, or all, of these brief posts to your students and show them the accompanying photograph.

Building upon some of the content from the first ten days, ask the students to think and reflect on this posts, and then answer these questions in their Genius Notebook:

1. What problem did these students face? How did they solve it? Would you say their action demonstrated genius thinking?

2. What traits of a genius leader and learner did these students exhibit? What is their genius?

3. Did these students have any extraordinary skill, knowledge or resources available to them that aren't available to most students? Or would it be reasonable to say that any student could accomplish what some of these students accomplished, if they are willing to put in the hard work, imagination and creativity necessary to make it happen?

Rachel Wheeler – Building Homes in Haiti

Rachel Wheeler, a sixth grader, was inspired to help those affected by the earthquake in Haiti. She explained to The Huffington Post, "You can't just sit around and think about doing it. You got to actually get out there and do it."

So she began working with Food for the Poor, which feeds people around the world, and worked to donate enough money to build 27 homes in an area hit hard by the earthquake.

Not satisfied with her initial efforts, she continued her fundraising and gathered enough support to rebuild a school destroyed during the earthquake.

Because of her efforts, 350 students attend a brand new school stocked with supplies. Rachel kept up her work with the goal of building an additional 20 homes, and she has raised a total of over $175,000 for the village.

http://www.huffingtonpost.com/2011/11/14/rachel-wheeler-food-for-poor_n_1093732.html

Dylan Siegel – Author and Fundraiser

When Dylan Siegel's best friend was diagnosed with a rare liver disease in 2012, Dylan decided to do something about it. He wrote a book called *Chocolate Bar*, because in his world, "that's so chocolate bar" is a high form of praise. This is because Dylan was six years old. He began selling copies of the book for $20 each.

Dr. David Weinstein, who leads the main team researching these diseases, thought it was a cute idea. But when sales of the book topped $400,000, Dr. Weinstein remarked, "[Dylan has] raised more money for this disease than all the medical foundations and all the grants combined. Ever."

The Global Genes Project, which advocates for rare disease research, honored Dylan and his friend with the RARE Champion Award—typically given to grown-ups.

Dylan didn't stop there. He designed other products for sale, and has now raised more than $1 million. Now 8, he vows not to stop raising money until the disease is cured.

"Kids can change the world just like any of us," Dr. Siegel told ABC News. http://www.chocolatebarbook.com, https://globalgenes.org

48

Mallory Fundora – Founder of Project Yesu

In the fall of 2010, 11-year-old Mallory Fundora put only one item on her Christmas wish list: she wanted money to help orphans from Uganda that she had met when their choir visited her church.

From this simple wish, Mallory became the founder of Project Yesu, a not-for-profit organization that provides food, medicine and education for children in Uganda. Through an array of fundraising activities, Project Yesu has raised more than $30,000. Her efforts were recognized by a resolution in the Tennessee House of Representatives, which deemed her "an intrepid young soul with extraordinary compassion."

Mallory says, "I want to show people what a difference one person can make…Kids have good ideas, and you know what? We don't know all the reasons why it won't work, we just know we what we want to do."

In the fall of 2013, Choose2Matter presented Mallory with the first Bammy Award for Student Initiative. She said that receiving a national award is the first thing that made teachers in her school take her efforts seriously:

From the time I started Project Yesu, only 3 out of 14 teachers ever showed any interest in what I am doing in Uganda…What about caring about students' passions? Showing interest in their lives? Encouraging them, finding their spark and helping them grow it, even if it doesn't make them better on a standardized test?"

To learn more, watch this video Mallory made about her travels in Uganda:

http://www.capitol.tn.gov/Bills/108/Bill/HJR0541.pdf

http://www.projectyesu.org, http://www.bammyawards.org/index.php

https://www.youtube.com/watch?v=InjWik6PlUs&feature=youtu.be

Kaitlin Brand – Published Video About Her Mother's Suicide

In a moving and courageous video, Kaitlin Brand, a 16-year-old from Grand Rapids, Michigan, shares her very personal message about suicide.

Although Kaitlin doesn't say a single word, her video speaks volumes, as she holds up pieces of paper explaining how she found her Mom hanging in her backyard after committing suicide.

Strong but humble, Kaitlin asks viewers to seek help if they are having suicidal thoughts.

The video resonated with viewers and soon went viral. Her story was picked up by news agencies across the country.

Even though her video has over 800,000 views, it's impossible to put a number on the impact of her simple act of courage. People around the world wrote to Kaitlin to share how she gave them the strength to deal with crises in their own lives, and it all started with a webcam and a story.

https://www.youtube.com/watch?v=InjWik6PlUs&feature=youtu.be

Katie Stagliano – Founder of Katie's Krops

After Katie Stagliano grew a 40-pound cabbage and fed people at a soup kitchen with her cabbage, she knew she had to do more. Even though Katie was in the third grade, she felt she could help others.

As Katie explains, "My dream is that there are no hungry people."

Since that time over five years ago, Katie has persuaded her high school to grow food and has worked with large organizations to grow food for soup kitchens. She recently published a children's book, *Katie's Cabbage*, that tells her story of generosity and hope. She has no plans to stop. As Katie says, "I want more people to get involved, more people to help in the fight against hunger. Growing vegetables is fun and it is so great to help people. If I can do it, anyone can."

http://katieskrops.com/home.html

http://www.amazon.com/Katies-Cabbage-Young-Palmetto-Books-ebook/dp/B00MGRV0IQ

Richard Turere – Inventor of "Lion Lights"

Having found his family's only bull dead after an attack from lions, Richard Turere, a 13-year-old from the Masai community in Kenya, felt there had to be a way to protect his family's livestock from the lions who roam over from Nairobi National Park. Yet he wanted to do so without killing or harming the lions, as many of his tribesmen did.

After fire and scarecrows failed to work, Richard took to walking around his cowshed with a torch. He realized that lions were afraid of moving light. Using parts from a broken flashlight and a motorcycle, he created solar powered flashing lights that kept the lions away from his family's cowshed. His invention has now been adopted at farms all over Kenya.

His invention earned him the chance to speak at the TED conference and a scholarship to Brookhouse International School in Kenya.

http://www.ted.com/speakers/richard_turere

Cassandra Lin – Co-Founder of Project T.G.I.F.

Cassandra Lin, a Westerly 7th grader, found the solution to many problems at once when she co-founded Project T.G.I.F. (Turn Grease Into Fuel).

While attending the Rhode Island Green Expo in 2008, Lin learned it is possible to turn cooking oil into biodiesel fuel. She was also aware that her community had a program for helping those in need with heating oil during the winter.

As Lin explained to Business Innovation Factory, she also knew that sewage pipes in her town were being clogged with the very cooking oil that could be turned into biodiesel. "We looked at an array of problems to see what we could solve in our own community."

To date, Project TGIF has donated over 29,000 gallons of BioHeat to local charities in Rhode Island, heating the homes of 290 local families, valued at over $120,000.

http://www.businessinnovationfactory.com/summit/innovator/cassandra-lin

http://www.projecttgif.com

Mikey Stolzenberg – Mikey's Run Raised $230,000 for Bombing Victims

After the Boston Marathon bombing in 2013, 13-year-old Mikey Stolzenberg wanted to help the survivors of the blast.

Mikey knew what the amputees would have to deal with. In 2008, his hands and feet were amputated in an effort to save his life from a skin infection that turned into septic shock, and then gangrene. Mikey decided to raise one million dollars to donate to the survivors of the bombing.

He and his 17-year-old brother Harris created Mikey's run and declared that Harris would run the 2014 Boston Marathon in exchange for donations to Boston's One Fund to support survivors of the bombing.

Even more extraordinary than Mikey's concern for others and his fundraising ability was the wisdom that this young teen shared.

Mikey spoke to the Sun Sentinel about how the people who lost limbs in the bombing would feel:

"First, they will be sad. They are losing something they will never get back, and it's scary. I was scared. But they'll be OK. They just don't know that yet."

http://mikeysrun.com

Malala Yousafzai – Fights for All Women to Have Access to Education

In October 2012, a member of Pakistan's Taliban tried to silence support for girls' access to education by shooting an outspoken, and well-spoken, proponent of women empowerment.

The person who so frightened the Taliban with her words was 15-year-old Malala Yousafzai.

Malala recovered from her injuries and is now bringing even greater attention to the issue of universal access to education.

July 12, 2013, Malala's 16th birthday, was declared "Malala Day" by the United Nations.

Malala delivered a powerful speech at the UN, in which she said:

"Let us pick up our books and pens. They are our most powerful weapons. One child, one teacher, one pen and one book can change the world. Education is the only solution."

In 2014, Malala became the youngest-ever Nobel Laureate when she was awarded the Nobel Peace Prize.

Malala celebrated her 18th birthday by opening a school for Syrian Refugee girls.

In a 2014 TED Talk, Malala's father, Ziauddin Yousafzai, told stories from his daughter's life. He said to the audience: "Why is my daughter so strong? Because I didn't clip her wings."

https://www.youtube.com/watch?v=3rNhZu3ttIU

http://www.nobelprize.org/nobel_prizes/peace/laureates/2014/yousafzai-facts.html

http://www.npr.org/sections/thetwo-way/2015/07/12/422358157/malala-turns-18-and-opens-a-school-for-syrian-refugee-girls

http://www.ted.com/talks/ziauddin_yousafzai_my_daughter_malala?language=en

Jack Andraka – Invented Cancer Detection Test

Jack Andraka was only 15 years old when he developed a novel way to test for pancreatic cancer after a family friend died of the disease.

In an inspiring TED Talk, Andraka explained how, even after 200 professors refused to work with him, he persevered in his efforts, "undeterred, due to my teenage optimism."

Approximately 40,000 people die a year from pancreatic cancer, because by the time symptoms are presented in patients it is often too late for doctors to help. Andraka's test may some day save tens of thousands of lives each year.

In 2012, Jack became the only high school freshman to win the $75,000 first prize at the Intel Science and Engineering Fair. He has since been profiled on CNN and 60 Minutes, and has had a personal audience with present and past US Presidents, as well as the Pope.

http://www.ted.com/speakers/jack_andraka

Discussion Questions for The World Needs Your Contribution:

- The authors provide examples of young people who are changing the world. Which one resonated the most with you? Which one did your students most identify with?
- Please share other remarkable examples of students changing the world, including any links to online information about their efforts.

I Am; You Are

Objective:

Students will increase their self-awareness and learn to notice and appreciate qualities of their classmates.

Background:

Describing the elements of your identity is not an easy task. We can help student build their self-awareness and engage in self-reflection.

This lesson helps students focus on the following aspects of self:

- What they especially like
- What they are proud of
- What impacts and moves them
- What they might like or wish to change
- Who influences them
- How they feel at the moment about their life

Materials:

A supply of mirrors equal to roughly half the students in the class.

Lesson:

Begin by explaining to students that they will be thinking about themselves and all the qualities they are proud of or love about themselves.

These qualities can be physical: Example, I am a great dancer. Or they could be inside qualities of their confidence or abilities. I am a loyal friend. I am sympathetic.

Remind students that this exercise is not about ego and bragging; it is about being proud your own strengths and recognizing the strengths in the genius learners and leaders around us.

1. Share that the way we are going to share how they feel, how they see ourselves and others is in the form of a poem.

- Write these two words on the board: I AM...
- The poems we create will be about 10 lines.
- There are no rules except that each stanza and statement will begin with "I am..."
- Statements can be positive, negative, or neutral, but they should be true.

2. Give an example of your own "I am..." poem.

I am a teacher.
I am a mom.
I am a wife.
I am a speaker.
I am a writer.
I am most happy when I am with children.
I am so proud of the students I teach.
I am grateful to be doing something I am so passionate about.
I am Mrs. Maiers.

3. Ask students to write ten "I am..." statements on their paper.

They can record this in their Genius Notebook or on paper. If they have trouble starting, suggest a few adjectives, nouns and descriptions based on your observations.

4. When each student has completed this, organize them to into pairs. Have students choose which partner will go first.

5. Pass out a mirror to each pair and have one partner be the listener and hold up the mirror so that the partner who is reading can see himself or herself in the mirror.

6. When you say to begin, have all of the readers read their poems out loud while looking directly at themselves in the mirror.

When everyone is finished, have them read their poem again, this time looking directly at their partner, not at themselves in the mirror.

Remind the students who are listening that it is ok to look into someone's eyes; it shows that you are interested in what they are saying, even if it feels a little uncomfortable.

7. Switch partners and repeat the process so every student has a chance to hear their poem.

Reflection Questions:

Have students debrief as a class or individually on the following:

- How did it make you feel to describe yourself?
- Do you like who you are?
- What would you not change about who you are? What do you want to change?
- How did it feel to read your poem while looking at yourself in the mirror? How did it feel to read it while looking at your partner?
- What did you learn about yourself?
- What did you learn about each other?

"You Are" Poems

Students will repeat the above process by writing a poem about their classmate based on what they learned and know.

Students gain confidence by identifying personal talents and practice they see in others. They work collaboratively and practice giving and receiving compliments verbally and in writing.

By identifying admirable qualities in others, students become more interested, appreciative, empathetic and supportive of one another.

To help ignite their curiosity and appreciation for one another have students practice giving and receiving compliments by describing positive aspects about their peers by having them stand by a chalkboard or large white board while the class shares positive qualities about their classmates.

After each student has had a chance to "take a seat," pair students up to write their poems with each line beginning: "You Are"

When students have finished writing their qualities that are most appreciated and valued about their partner, have both partners come up and share in front of the class.

Reflection Questions:

- How did it feel to share these qualities with your partner?
- Why did you choose these words or qualities?
- Was it harder to write about yourself or to hear what others wrote about you?
- How did hearing your poem feel?
- What surprised you most about what your partner said?

Discussion Questions for I Am; You Are:

- Why do we build student's self-awareness and help them engage in self-reflection?
- What is the difference between bragging about your ego and being proud of your own strengths? How did you differentiate these two viewpoints with your students?
- How did the poem process contribute to unleashing your student's genius?
- What was different about the students writing poems about themselves versus writing poems about their classmates? Overall, how did this affect your class dynamics?

Self-Awareness

Objective:

Students will understand self-awareness.

Background:

This book emphasizes *process, not projects*. If students can navigate the process of learning, they can successfully achieve a wide range of outcomes. That's why it's vital to cultivate in them the skill of self-awareness.

Self-awareness is process. It reveals to students their own strengths, weaknesses, and behaviors. It gives them the power to learn and change independently in real-time.

One of the great benefits of Genius Hour is that students drive their own learning. This requires that they think ahead, plan, and react to change.

A common worry about starting Genius Hour is how to manage 25+ unique geniuses, all learning different content and pursuing diverse passions. Instilling self-awareness in students is key to making this transition.

The first lesson below gets students to think critically about their own individual traits. Students will answer from a list of open-ended questions as they explore what makes them unique.

The second lesson serves as an introduction to managing their brain's executive functions—the "command and control" center in the prefrontal cortex. This activity shows students how to listen to the inner thoughts they experience as they work and to understand how those thoughts can both engage and distract them.

Self-awareness is a skill that is never fully mastered. However, with continual practice, students develop habits that allow them to work and learn without someone—often their teacher—looking over their shoulder.

Lesson:

Part 1: (~20 minutes)

Class, who do you think has the biggest effect on how much you learn?

[React to the responses]

*Those are all excellent responses. Everyone you mentioned has a big impact on your learning and your success. However, I want you to know that the most important person to your learning . . . is **you**! You have the most power over the things you want to accomplish.*

But, just knowing that fact doesn't mean a whole lot just yet. This knowledge is like a tool that you need to learn how to use. Let me give you an example.

What are some tools that people use every day?

(Answer several responses. When you land on a good response, use it to further your discussion. I'll use a computer for our example.)

A computer, that's a very good example of a tool. Now, if you had never used a computer before and someone just gave one to you and said, "Here you go," would you know what to do with it? It would be pretty difficult, right? You would have to know how to plug it in, how to turn it on, and what different applications do.

You are a bit like that computer. The more you know about how you work, the more you are able to do. Today, we are going to do just that.

Bring their attention to their notes from the previous lesson, "I Am, You Are."

Here we have a list of statements that follow the words, "I Am."

Take a look at all these statements.

Now ask yourself this question - which may be the hardest one you've ever answered: "What Makes Me, Me?"

You may have a lot of different answers to this question. Some of them you can express in writing, while others might work well with a drawing, a poem, or whatever you think works best.

In a minute, you are going to provide a variety of answers. Try to do a few that seem easy and a few that seem hard. Keep working until I say, "Stop."

Allow 10 minutes for students to work on the list. This is a great time to walk around the room and ask questions about their responses. You'll gain some amazing insights!

Have students share one interesting thing they wrote/created.

Part 2: (~20 minutes)

Wow, I am amazed at everything I saw around the room. The next step in learning more about how we work is to look at what we'll call our "inner voice." Let me explain what the inner voice is.

When I read, there is silent conversation going on. In my head, I hear a voice reading the words. It lets me know if I am reciting the words accurately and that they sound like I am talking aloud and not robotic.

But another voice I am aware of and attend to is the voice that talks to and interacts with the writer. This is the voice that helps me understand the words I hear myself reciting. I call that my inner voice, because it is like I am having the conversation with the author inside my head. Thinking about the writer in this way helps me interact with the ideas in the book.

However, the inner voice is there more than just when we read. Our inner voice is also there when you wake up in the morning and think to yourself, "I'm really excited for today"—or perhaps "I'm still tired and want to go back to bed." Your inner voice is there when you're

working really hard on something and it says, "Come on, just a little bit longer. Keep going.

That inner voice is there when you're happy or sad, when you're tired or full of energy, when you're alone or with other people.

Share a story of your own inner voice.

Take a moment and think about a time when you had that inner voice talking inside.

Pause for a few moments, and then ask for a few students to share. Ask them if the voice had any effect on how they felt or what they did.

The most important thing to know about your inner voice is that you have control over it. You can choose the things your voice says. And, most importantly, what your voice says has an impact on how you act. The more positive things that your inner voice says, the more you are able to learn and be the best you can be. That's why you are going to plan for what your inner voice will say at different times.

Discussion Questions for Self-Awareness:

- *Liberating Genius* emphasizes process, not projects; what is the difference between the two and how do you explain this to your students?
- How does this two-part lesson develop self-awareness and re-veal students' strengths, weaknesses, and behaviors?
- Why do you think it is important for students to drive their own learning during Genius Hour?
- How do these lessons build a foundation for Genius Hour? What has worked well and what still needs scaffolding?

Days 14 through 20:
Acting Through Collective
Genius

Finding A Dream Team

Objective:

Students will identify role models who exemplify sharing your Genius.

Background:

Each of us possesses the ability to achieve greatness in our lives. Each of us can learn a lot from individuals who have distinguished themselves by accomplishing something great and extraordinary, just as we discussed a few weeks ago in "How do Genius Leaders Work."

There are so many people who have inspired me—people I consider in many ways to be special, intelligent, and brilliant. These extraordinary people have taught me by example in the ways they learn and lead.

Here's the amazing thing, I have never even met most of these people in person. I call these people my Dream Team. They are individuals I have deliberately selected to be inspired by and whose actions and behaviors I would like to reflect in terms of my own dreams and goals.

I have learned that you don't have to know people personally for them to be role models. Your Dream Team can be composed of someone famously great, like any of the people we learned about during our jigsaw activity, or of a special individual, a coach or a teacher whom you want to be more like when you grow up.

A good role model doesn't have to be someone famous or popular at the moment. A role model can be someone in your family, school, or community; someone whose actions you respect and whose behaviors and habits inspire you. But you may wonder how to identify such an individual. Here are some things you can think about as you select someone for your role model:

- What makes this individual interesting?
- What is special about this individual?
- What characteristics does this individual possesses? How do you know?

I have designed an activity, the Dream Team Selection Procedure, that will help you identify one or more real-life mentors whom you may want to emulate. Write the answers, and put them away to review later.

The Dream Team Selection Procedure consists of four topics that encourage students to reflect on the qualities of individuals they consider for role models. For example, the third topic asks them to identify one trait that stands out for the selected individual.

Here it is important for students to understand that, for example, Michael Jordan did not win games because he was a great basketball player; he was a master of self-awareness and perseverance, which propelled his talent to a legendary level. You want students to recognize that it was Einstein's insatiable curiosity that changed the field of science. Similarly, if not for Walt Disney's audacious imagination, there would be no Disney World.

Lesson:

Ask students to do the following:

- Create a list of five people with whom you've achieved a kind of success together, or someone who supported you in accomplishing something.
- Next to each person's name, list the qualities you value most about that person. Be specific.
- Reflect on all those qualities you've listed. Now select one key attribute that stands out above the others.

Next, select your top *two* choices to share with the class as the best possible candidates for the class Dream Team.

The most important thing you need to be clear about is the reason you selected these people. You should know exactly what skills, behaviors, habits, or attitudes you think make that individual extraordinary.

For example, everyone knows that Albert Einstein was extraordinary. The important question to ask and answer is, what traits did Einstein have that made him a genius?

Discussions Questions for Finding A Dream Team:

- Explain in your words why identifying a Dream Team is important?
- Reflect on how your students created their Dream Team, what challenges did they face? What triumphs did they embrace?
- How do you think the development of this team supports your students in liberating their genius?

What Matters to the People Around Me

Objective:

Students will reflect on what is happening around them and learn what matters most to others.

Background:

Class, we've looked at what is happening in the world around us. This could be in our neighborhood, city, state, our country and the world. I want you to take out your Genius Notebook. Read through the things we've been learning about. I want you to share five events with a partner and tell why these are so important – give at least one sentence. Partners should ask the following questions about the event:

- *Why is it so important? Why did I write this down in my Genius Notebook?*
- *Who does this affect and how?*
- *What happens if no one does anything to help?*
- *How does it affect me?*
- *What have people or organization done to help this?*

Set timer for 15 minutes and walk around room, listening to students' ideas.

Now that you've had time to share and discuss, I want you to choose two that you think are the most important. Write them on a post-it and place them up here on our chart paper.

As students are doing this, ask students to see if they can start categorizing the events that are being posted up.

Wow! So much great thinking class! Let's look at how we categorized these events. Why did we choose these categories? (Have discussion on a few of these)

Now, let's look at the events you've listed. Let's talk about the events and why you think they are so important. (Have discussion on a few of these)

I'm so proud of all the hard work you've put into this. We didn't get through all of them, but we'll revisit this chart. I want you to now think about the events and what others are trying to do to solve the problems that relate to them. What do you notice about the solutions? What ideas do you have that could help? (Write on board)

I want you to access your Genius Notebook. For one of the events you wrote on your post it, write about these two questions that I posed to you. What do you notice about the solutions? Are people even trying to help? What ideas do you have that could help? This is genius work.. This is when you need to use your brain to think of solutions as well as unique ways to help. I'll give you 5 minutes to work on this.

We did a whole lot of sharing and thinking today! Thank you for your contribution. We'll continue this conversation tomorrow.

Discussion Questions for What Matters to the People Around Me:

- Why do you think discussing what matters to others is important?
- How do these books and stories support discussions about what matters to the characters? What personal stories or additional resources have you supplemented this lesson with?
- What were some surprising responses or conversations that surfaced during this lesson? What prompted them to develop?

Many Kinds of Courage

Objective:

The student will explore and appreciate the many kinds of courage and to develop an understanding that ordinary people can experience courage in many unique ways.

"By acting, we make things concrete; action breeds motivation, not the other way around."

-Todd Henry, Author, The Accidental Creative

Background:

Being brave is hard work. You can be brave, or you can be comfortable, but you can't be both. You have to choose. There are so many images of what brave looks like in real life and learning.

- Is it running into a burning building?
- Is it speaking up when someone else needs you to?
- It is saving a hurt animal?
- Is it trying to defy the impossible?

In his fantastic book, *Courage,* Bernard Waber explores the many varied kinds of courage and celebrates the moments, big and small, that bring out the hero in each of us.

I use this book to launch a deep conversation about what courage is and what it is not.

Here is the publisher's note:

What is courage? Certainly it takes courage for a firefighter to rescue someone trapped in a burning building, but there are many other kinds of courage too. Everyday kinds that normal, ordinary people exhibit all the time, like "being the first to make up after an argument," or "going to bed without a nightlight." Bernard Waber explores the many varied kinds of courage and celebrates the moments, big and small, that bring out the hero in each of us.

Ask students work in groups and discuss the following question: What is courage?

Invite students to come up with their own definition of courage and share that definition "courageously" with their classmates.

Students can use any medium or mode to communicate their understanding of the concept: Writing, drawing, acting out, video clips, etc.

Compare and contrast the examples presented in the book with the examples students shared with one another.

- How do you think Bernard Waber is defining courage?
- How is this alike/different than how we see the word?

Quotation Cards

Share with students the following quotation cards; each with a different quote about how courage is defined in the world.

Have them regroup and compare/contrast these definitions of courage with those previously discussed including their own.

"It takes a great deal of bravery to stand up to our enemies, but just as much to stand up to our friends." — J.K. Rowling, Harry Potter and the Sorcerer's Stone	"Courage is the most important of all the virtues because without courage, you can't practice any other virtue consistently." — Maya Angelou
"It takes courage to grow up and become who you really are." — E.E. Cummings	"Courage is resistance to fear, mastery of fear - not absence of fear." — Mark Twain
"Believe you can and you're halfway there." — Theodore Roosevelt	"Courage doesn't always roar. Sometimes courage is the little voice at the end of the day that says I'll try again tomorrow." — Mary Anne Radmacher

As a class, synthesize the conversation by coming up with an agreed upon and working definition of the word courage.

As both a reflection and reminder, you can distribute the following graphic organizer or have students reflect in a journal on the many kinds of courage they explored today and will see in the world.

Many Kinds of Courage
My Reflection by_____

"There are many kinds of courage.
Awesome kinds.
And everyday kinds.
Still, courage is courage—
Whatever kind."

What is **your** best example of courage?
Describe it in a sentence.

Courage is:

Explain why this is an example of courage is important you.

Set a courage goal:

Describe what you are going to do to act and be braver than you are
and as brave as you can be here:

Discussion Questions for Many Kinds of Courage:

- Why do you think being brave is an important step for liberating your genius?
- Share your class' working definition of the word, **courage**? Describe in your own words, how did you come up with this definition?

How To Collaborate Effectively

Objective:

Students will understand that we are smarter together; that their contribution is expected and needed and will learn to value and honor the contribution of others.

Background:

"Collaboration" has become a buzzword that we attach to any process that involves people working together. This is because we often use collaboration as a synonym for other buzzwords that start with C: Co-operation, Communication and Coordination.

In doing so, we miss the most critical element – **value creation**.

Collaboration describes a process of value creation that our traditional structures of communication and teamwork can't achieve.

Let's break it down further and clarify what it really is.

Collaboration has three parts: Team, Process, and Purpose

1. Two or more people (Team)

2. Working together (Process)

3. Towards shared goals (Purpose)

A group of people using social software together doesn't, by itself, translate into collaboration.

Technology certainly raises the bar of what is possible, but merely using them does not create value.

We say that because I see schools and organizations struggling to fit social technologies into their culture. Widespread platform or tool adoption is not enough. There needs to be a unified plan, an understanding of what these tools can and can't do, and more importantly how people are going to work together.

Great tools available can facilitate such collaboration, but even the best tools cannot guarantee that success.

Collaboration:

- Must be embedded in the culture, where a standard and expectation ethic of contribution flourishes.
- People in the classroom or community must recognize they are smarter together.
- People must work "out loud" – sharing is constant.
- People collectively solve problems.
- Together, everyone discovers more innovative ways to be successful.

Now this sounds high-tech, but it happens elegantly every day in kindergarten classrooms, where we call it "Show and Tell."

We learned how to collaborate in the sandbox with friend and strangers alike – now we get to expand the size of the sandbox and extend the invitation for creation to anyone, living anyplace, anytime, anywhere.

This is where and how disruption happens – when you invite people into the room and assure them that their contribution will be honored, they choose to contribute. They choose collaboration.

Tap into a crowd if you believe the most valuable person *is* the crowd. You must innately believe that smartest person in the room *is* the room – and that the more diverse room, the smarter it gets.

Collaboration requires unrelenting determination and commitment from those who now understand that the desired result can only be achieved together.

People at any level can make an impact, be a leader, break a barrier. No only can they; they must.

We are smarter together.

Further reading: "The Smartest Person in the Room is the Room."

http://www.angelamaiers.com/2013/02/the-smartest-person-in-the-room-is-the-room-so-whos-on-your-invite-list

Lesson:

Playground talk

Discuss how people collaborate on the playground or in the sandbox.

- For younger students, ask how it currently happens
- For older students, ask how it did happen

Ask students, *"When you are on the swings and they are all taken, how do you know who gets to use them?"* This should prompt a discussion of issues of fairness, informal cooperation, and inclusiveness

What are the rules for tag? Who decided this? What if you disagree about whether someone is out or not? Again, this should result in a discussion about Rules; fairness; cooperation

When you head out to the playground, how do you decide where you are going to play? This may prompt a discussion about individual talents and preferences.

Reveal to students how all their responses show that they *already* have an important skill needed to be successful as students and as adults: collaboration

"When you have a tough problem in front of you, remember the playground"

Once the activity is over, have older students read "The Sandbox Manifesto," younger students can watch the video embedded in it. Ask students if they agree with the points raised in this article or video.

http://www.angelamaiers.com/2014/10/the-sandbox-manifesto

Active Collaboration

Sometimes in school, the work you do is on your own. However, the work of geniuses is often working with others. Doing genius work means doing big, challenging things, and that requires that we put our brains together. It requires that we collaborate. (Define "collaborate" for students in younger grades.)

Do you want to know a fun secret? Collaborating and working together is something that many adults have trouble with. They try to do things on their own, and they aren't able to accomplish as much. However, from what I heard from our discussion of the playground, it's obvious that you all have a lot of experience collaborating.

Let's do a quick example to put this into action.

Put students into small groups of about 4-5. Each group should have access to this Arranging Sentences Activity:

Arrange these sentences into a paragraph that makes sense to your group.

- The traveler went to another worker and asked again, "What are you doing?"
- It's about the mission everyone shares.

- The third worker responded, "Can't you see, we're building a cathedral."
- He asked the first person he saw, "I'm not from this village. What is everyone doing?"
- With this, the traveler learned that the work you do is about more than just one task.
- The worker replied, "Can't you see, I'm earning money to support my family."
- A traveler came to a village and saw many people working.
- The person replied, "Can't you see, I'm cutting stone into large blocks."
- Not satisfied, the traveler went on to a third worker and asked yet again, "What are you doing?"

Original paragraph

A traveler came to a village and saw many people working. He asked the first person he saw, "I'm not from this village. What is everyone doing?" The person replied, "Can't you see, I'm cutting stone into large blocks." The traveler went to the next worker and asked again, "What are you doing?" The worker replied, "Can't you see, I'm earning money to support my family." Not satisfied, the traveler went on to a third worker and asked yet again, "What are you doing?" The third worker responded, "Can't you see, we're building a cathedral." With this, the traveler learned that the work you do is about more than just one task. It's about the mission everyone shares.

Have groups complete the activity, which should only take a few minutes. When they are done, talk to them about how they completed the activity:.

- *What did your group do to get the task done?*
- *What steps did you take?*
- *Did people take on roles or assign roles?*
- *Were there disagreements? How did you handle them?*
- *What connections can you make between this activity and how you collaborate on the playground?*

78

Encourage dialogue about the collaboration process. Get students to reflect on their recent actions.

Connecting school to the world

Tell students that throughout their lives they will be called on to contribute their genius to solve big problems. However, solving them isn't as easy as arranging sentences, e.g. to getting food to people to eat, you need farmers, truck drivers, grocers, chefs, safety inspectors, etc. They all collaborate, and they all contribute their genius.

Have students identify a general problem to be solved:

- It can be small, like a broken drinking fountain in their school
- It can be big, like people not having a place to sleep

Have students identify how their geniuses could contribute

Have students identify what contributions from others they would need

Discussions Questions for How to Collaborate Effectively:

- What does collaboration look and feel like in your classroom?
- Describe how your students experience the process of **value creation**?
- How would you explain how disruption happens? What does it do to your collaborative groups?
- How does this lesson incorporate or draw on previous lessons?
- Compare and contrast the work that you do as an individual versus the work you accomplish with others?
- What were some big takeaways that your students experienced after piecing together the sentences to create a logical paragraph?
- When identifying a general problem to be solved, how did you encourage students to collaborate, contribute and leverage their genius?

Finding Mentors and Collaborators

Many scholars of the past burrowed into library stacks, read the printed literature on a topic, consulted with a mentor, and emerged with their research.

Today, the smartest person in the room is the room.

While there are many instances of scholarly collaboration throughout history, none rise to the level of what's possible today, where dozens or scores or hundreds of people from around the world can connect simultaneously and in real-time.

NYU Professor Clay Shirky says that most people "over estimate the value of access to information and underestimate the value of access to each other."

While this may be true of most adults, students already understand the power and value of connecting to others, and they are exceedingly comfortable doing it digitally.

Students dominate popular Q&A sites such as Yahoo! Answers, Answers.com and Quizlet. However, these sites are not authoritative, rarely provide links to references, and should not be cited as a source for a student paper.

Fortunately, students can explore many free avenues online to connect with experts in almost any field of study or area of interest. All they need is for adults to open the door and point them in the right direction.

What Could Go Wrong?

- When students interact with adults online, there is always the possibility of inappropriate interaction.

- The role of adults is to teach students to navigate online safely, and these sites provide excellent learning opportunities not found anywhere else.

- All of these resources are moderated to some degree, so when using them, students should be mindful, not afraid.

- Just as when a teen ventures into the big city for the first time without adult supervision, they need to be aware of their surroundings and take precautions.

- Always have an open line of communication with your students concerning their online research.

Here are examples of places where students can ask questions of research or subject matter experts online, and possibly find a mentor or collaborator.

1. Ask a Librarian

Many local, county and college libraries offer a virtual "Ask a Librarian" service through which a student can ask a trained librarian for reference help. Many libraries work through a network of libraries to provide 24/7 coverage around the world. When a student needs to find a great resource but can't arrange a face-to-face visit with a reference librarian, Ask a Librarian services fill the gap.

2. Quora

Quora is a Question and Answer site that is comprised mostly of professionals. Unlike other Q&A sites, most users register with their real name and provide their credentials, and most answers are at least somewhat useful.

We recently created this Choose2Matter page on Quora; when a student asks a question about social entrepreneurship, we'll find an expert to answer it. https://www.quora.com/topic/Choose2Matter

3. Twitter

With hundreds of millions of users, Twitter can be an excellent resource for students to find that handful of people who can provide them insight.

Students need to learn to use "hashtags" to target their Tweets to people likely to have knowledge about the subject of their question.

When Maggie Moran, a sophomore education major, wanted to find an expert to discuss tutoring a student with interrupted formal education (SIFE), she turned to Twitter, using the #SIFE hashtag. She reports that, "within minutes of my tweet, I received five replies with suggestions on books to read, methods to try, and educators to follow who were experts in the area."

4. Yoursphere

Yoursphere is a safe destination where students can connect with other students around their "spheres" of interest. Teachers can also create a classroom "home page" where they can share content and interact with students, and other classrooms.

http://yoursphere.com/form/330124/educators

5. Video Conferencing

Services such as Skype make it feasible for anyone with an Internet connection to video conference, free of charge, with anyone else, anywhere in the world, who also has an Internet connection. Skype in the Classroom offers premium tools free of charge to educators, including a service to connect with guest authors, expert teachers, and others. https://education.microsoft.com/skypeintheclassroom

This article discusses how teachers all across the globe are using video conferencing to connect their students with eyewitnesses to history, government leaders, authors, and other inspiring adults.

http://www.findingdulcinea.com/news/education/2013/Skype.html

Lesson:

Ask students to reflect on Clay Shirky's statement that most people "over estimate the value of access to information and underestimate the value of access to each other." Ask them what this means to them.

Then, discuss each of the above services with students and ask for what purpose, and when, they might use each one.

Depending on the age and sophistication of your students, either create a classroom account or have students create individual accounts for each of the services (or divide the services up among the students, so that each one is used by 1/5 of your class).

Then submit several questions or inquiries or offers to connect and collaborate to each of the above services and wait several days for responses to flow in.

Then, meet with your class to discuss the responses.

When this exercise is done, ask them once again to reflect on Clay Shirky's statement at the top of this lesson. Have their views of the relative value of access to information and to other people changed?

Discussions Questions for Mentors and Collaborators:

- Reflect on Clay Shirky's quote about over estimating the value of access to information. Why is this important to consider and discuss? What emerged in your conversation with your students when asking what this meant to them?
- How will your students find these digital platforms useful when asking research questions to mentors and collaborators online?
- Have their views of the relative value of access to information and other people changed? Why or why not?

Sharing Our Genius With the World

Objective:

Students will understand the importance of sharing their Genius with the world outside of their classroom, and will learn tools that will enable them to do so.

Background:

Show students that you take their ideas seriously and believe there is a global audience for those ideas. In time, students will believe the same.

If students have an idea, however big or small or crazy or epic or outlandish, we ask that they write it down, pursue it and most importantly, share it with others.

Sharing your idea and asking for help can change everything. We practiced sharing our needs and gives and used every new and emerging technology to ensure this happened.

Additional reading: Juliet Revell, Book Creator Brings Out the Genius in Our Classroom:

http://www.redjumper.net/blog/2014/04/book-creator-brings-genius-classroom/

Lesson:

The "You Matter Manifesto" begins by telling the reader "You are enough." It is a clarion call to everyone to step up and into their genius and contribute it to the world.
http://www.choose2matter.org/manifesto/

Display on a digital screen that the whole class can see, or print out copies of it. Have students take turns, one at a time, reading one tenet of the Manifesto, and additional material, to the class. Then discuss each tenet of the Manifesto, one by one. For each one, ask students what the words mean to them.

Next, to bring in a real-life example of finding the courage to share your genius with the world, have the students read "Writing that is WOW - Worthy of the World" - or if you're short on time, just play the video embedded in the lesson.

http://www.angelamaiers.com/2015/03/writing-that-is-wow-worthy-of-the-world/

Again, ask students to share their takeaways from watching this video.

Next, assign students to write their reflections in their Genius Notebooks, and to then share this content with the world.

Don't limit students to the written word; student "output" may be a video documentary, a podcast, a traditional paper, a series of photographs, a work of art, a Sway, an Office Mix presentation or an oral presentation.

https://sway.com, https://mix.office.com/en-us/Home

Students can import content from their OneNote Genius Hour notebook to the web with Sway.com and build a beautiful, interactive presentations for each project.

Here are just a few of the platforms that students can use:

- Yoursphere is a student-friendly sharing space. Educators can create their own classroom, post prompts and have students respond right on the class page. The page can be viewed by other approved classrooms on Yoursphere.

- Some students may embark on a project that will take the full-school year - and perhaps the next one as well. Others may work on a series of short projects. They can save and publish their presentations at Docs.com, a free sharing/publishing tool powered by Microsoft. In later editions of this book, we'll introduce a way for students to use Docs.com to finding students with whom they might collaborate. https://docs.com/en-us

- On Padlet each student can share their reflections on an electronic sticky note.

- Kidblog offers class blogs or individual student accounts.

Discussion Questions for Sharing Our Genius with the World:

- Why have students share their genius with the world?
- How did students respond to the real-life example of finding the courage to share their genius with the world? What were their takeaways?
- What tools or platforms did your students use to project their genius? How did these tools enhance their proclamation?

Putting It All Together

Objective:

We take a quick look back at the previous 19 days of genius work to help the students reflect on how they've grown as learners and leaders.

Background:

You and your students have put an enormous amount of time, energy, and heart and soul into the work over the past four weeks.

This will all be worth it, because Genius Hour is an apprenticeship to citizenship,

- Yes, students are now ready to work on a project.
- Yes they will learn how to better leverage technology.
- Yes, they will apply concepts used in math and science and reading.
- Yes, at the end, or some interim stopping point, many of the students will deliver some form of presentation that will exceed the great expectations that you or their parents had for them.

This all matters, but we can't miss the bigger picture.

Lesson:

Ask your students to take 15 minutes to read through their Genius Notebook, starting with Day 1.

Next, if at all possible, gather your students in a tight group. This is a celebration - we don't want them sitting in symmetrical rows with their feet planted on the floor in front of them. We want them to be able to feel and feed off the collective energy in the room. If your classroom is not suitable for this, consider whether there is an alternative space that would work.

Also, consider joining together with other classrooms that may have gone through Genius Hour at the same time. Don't limit yourself to the same grade! Sixth graders LOVE to hear second graders share their reflections on material that they have all been study, and vice-versa.

In the event that students start repeating each other, or focusing on the same narrow slices of the lessons, be ready to prompt them to discuss areas they've been ignoring.

Use prompts such as these:
- What has your Genius Notebook come to mean to you? Do you think you may want to keep it for many years, to see how you grow as a learner?
- How have you changed the way you work as a result of this learning?
- How has this course changed the way you view yourself and your place in the world?
- How have you changed what you aspire to be?
- Have you changed the way you view genius? What did you learn about the way that geniuses learn and work? Do you think you can emulate them?
- What was the most interesting thing that you've learned about yourself by using Thrively?
- Did you learn anything that surprised you about your classmates, your parents, or other people in the world?
- Have you changed the way you view courage? Has this made you more courageous?

- Do you believe that your work is worthy of the world, and that you have an obligation to share your work with others?
- Do you now believe this statement: "You are a genius, and the world needs your contribution?"

Discussions Questions for Putting It All Together:

- What does the phrase mean to you: Genius Hour is an apprenticeship to citizenship?
- How did you celebrate your students' accomplishments? What did you do to avoid narrowing in on specific lessons and instead focus on the bigger picture?
- How did the prompts and questions in this section help support your students overall reflection of their experience?
- What were some of the feelings and emotions that you and your class felt while reflecting on the Genius Hour journey?
- Looking back as an educator, was there anything you would have done differently? If so, what? What went well? What were some of your biggest hurdles? Why?
- Will you do Genius Hour again with another class? Why or why not?

Genius Hour

Why Passion Matters & How Genius Hour Cultivates It

There is a passion gap in education, and students are falling through it and drowning in ennui. Why does passion matter? What is the downside of an education system that does not encourage and nurture passion?

Bob Hurley, Sr., the boy's basketball coach at St. Anthony's High School in Jersey City, NJ, is one of the most successful coaches in American history. His teams have won 27 state championships and have produced five first-round NBA draft picks.

In his memoir, *Chasing Perfect,* Hurley discussed the most important quality he looks for in a new basketball player. You might have guessed his answer would be height, or speed, or ball-handling ability, or court sense.

His answer? Passion. Hurley explains:

"More times than not, Success Comes From An Ordinary Person with An extraordinary Desire To Be Successful, Rather Than A Person with Talent Who Doesn't Know What To Do With It"

Bob Hurley → Hall of Fame Coach

More times than not success comes from an ordinary person with an extraordinary desire to be successful, rather than a person with talent who doesn't know what to do with it."

Many others, in other professions, see passion as one of the most desirable traits in employees in the 21st century. New York Times columnist Thomas Friedman declares:

"We need everyone to be innovating new products and services to employ the people who are being liberated from routine work by automation and software. The winners won't just be those with more I.Q. It will also be those with more P.Q. (passion quotient) and C.Q. (curiosity quotient) to leverage all the new digital tools to not just find a job, but to invent one or reinvent one, and to not just learn but to relearn for a lifetime."

http://www.nytimes.com/2013/01/30/opinion/friedman-its-pq-and-cq-as-much-as-iq.html?_r=2

Many people mistake passion for an emotion, something people like to do in their spare time. Those are hobbies. Passion is what you must do, even if you have to suffer to do it. Passion is the genius of all geniuses. It's discipline at a level we can't comprehend.

So if passion is so essential in the work world, how do we cultivate it – in our children, our students, and our employees?

First of all, we must let them know that we expect they will accomplish great things.

In our Choose2Matter LIVE events in schools around the country, we lay the foundation of great expectations by opening with a bold statement to the students:

You are a genius, and the world needs your contribution.

https://www.smore.com/8un8-choose2matter-live

This is not a feel good statement. It is an invitation, and an expectation. We also establish that there is only one rule: **Be Brave**.

Next, we support them, every step of the way. To release a passion, a person may need above all else a role model. It may be a parent, a coach, a teacher, or a mentor.

Fred Wilson, a visionary venture capitalist, explains:

"Finding your passion is critical to having a full and fulfilling life. You have to put yourself in a place to do that. For me, it started with a woman ... who pushed me to 'figure it out' and it ended with a couple of guys who passed their passion on to me. I am sure there are many other ways to get there. But it won't happen without help. So surround yourself with people who care about you and listen to them. And good things will come from that."

What if you can't support them? At the very least, stay out of their way.

At a 2014 TED Talk, Ziauddin Yousafzai spoke about his daughter Malala, the 16yo Pakistani activist who was shot by the Taliban for standing up for the right of women to be educated. She subsequently gave an unforgettable speech before the United Nations.

https://www.youtube.com/watch?v=QRh_30C8l6Y

Mr. Yousafzai told the TED audience:

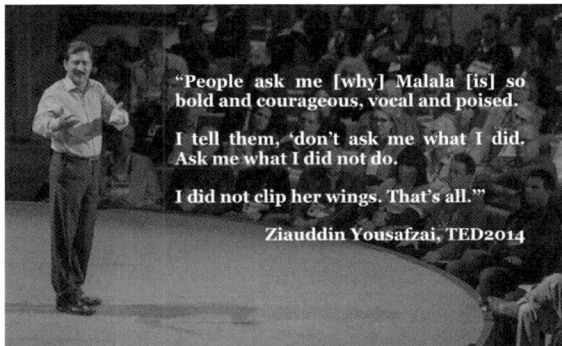

"People ask me [why] Malala [is] so bold and courageous, vocal and poised.

I tell them, 'don't ask me what I did. Ask me what I did not do.

I did not clip her wings. That's all.'"

Ziauddin Yousafzai, TED2014

http://www.ted.com/talks/ziauddin_yousafzai_my_daughter_malala

Sir Ken Robinson writes:

"Passion is a deep attraction for…. whatever fires your imagination and stokes your energy. We all have different aptitudes and we have unique passions. The challenge is to find them because it's in the fusion of both that we live our best lives."

Let's together help others find the fusion of their aptitudes and passions to live their best lives.

http://sirkenrobinson.com/page/5/

You'll Never Walk Alone:
The #GeniusHour Community

The decision to introduce Genius Hour into your classroom is a big step. You will not walk this way alone. You will be part of a community of tens of thousands of other Genius Hour teachers. They generously share their experiences, so that you can mimic their successes and learn more their mistakes.

The idea to bring Genius Hour into school crystallized for me in 2010 when Amy Sandvold and I were writing *The Passion-Driven Classroom*, a book that bridges the passion gap in school. In our book, we wrote of students working on passion projects. The following year, Daniel Pink was one of the first to coin the term "Genius Hour" in his book "Drive." He discussed its implementation within several companies in a 2011 blog post.

After watching a talk by Daniel Pink in November 2011, I sent this Tweet:

Angela Maiers
@AngelaMaiers

LOVE This! We need to have a "genius hour" in school- for teachers and students! #authorspeak11

Four months after I sent my first Tweet about Genius Hour, a group of teachers started a Genius Hour Twitter chat to exchange ideas and experiences.

A year later, four of them published "The Genius Hour Manifesto."

Hugh McDonald wrote, *"This was something special that engaged learners like nothing I had seen before. The learning atmosphere felt amazing. I could walk down the hall ... and return to see them all still on task, questioning, driving their own learning and having fun being curious."*
https://hughtheteacher.wordpress.com/category/genius-hour/

Gallit Zvi echoed some of the same themes: *"Student engagement is at its highest. Some students are huddled around a laptop doing research on countries, others are creating websites or presentations, and some are filming movies. Some are building and creating things with their hands. The common thread is that it is something they are passionate about and/or wonder about."*
https://hughtheteacher.wordpress.com/category/genius-hour/

Denise Krebs wrote, *"In this age where knowledge is ubiquitous and no longer belongs to the teacher to dispense during lesson plans, school needs to change. We need to inspire students to become life-long learners. Genius hour can do that."*

Joy Kirr was featured in a CNN article, which quoted one of her students who was upset that a snow day meant missing Genius Hour: *"It's definitely the highlight of my week. It's not a project a teacher assigned, it's something that actually interests you, and it gets you learning in different ways from what we do the rest of the day at school."*

Below, we offer advice from some of our favorite educators who have successfully introduced genius hour into their classrooms.

- In early 2015, a group of passionate #GeniusHour educators participated in a Twitter Chat in a Q&A Format. The insight shared is essential reading for any educator starting, or restarting, Genius Hour. This Storify captures the questions and many of the best answers from this Twitter chat. https://hughtheteacher.wordpress.com/category/genius-hour/

- Regularly check the #GeniusHour hashtag on Twitter to find great resources and advice from other educators all day, every day. There is also a monthly Twitter chat held on the first Thursday of each month at 9 pm Eastern Time / 6 pm Pacific.

- Some of our favorite videos or Slide Decks that introduce Genius Hour:

    o "What's It All About," by AJ Jiuliani
      https://vimeo.com/66324892

    o "What is Genius Hour" by ChrisKesler[MT2]

      http://www.slideshare.net/gallit_z/rscon4-presentation-on-genius-hour

    o "Genius Hour. Creativity. Passion. Wonder." by Gallit Zvi

      http://www.slideshare.net/gallit_z/rscon4-presentation on-genius-hour

- When creating materials for students, whether for Genius Hour or otherwise - draw some inspiration from this eye-opening post[MT3] in which one of AJ Jiuliani's students took AJ's handout that explained Genius Hour and completely redesigned it, with student-friendly, eye-popping graphics.

  http://ajjuliani.com/genius-hour-guidelines-re-designed-by-student/

- Denise Krebs, Gallit Zvi and Joy Kirr, three of the educators with whom I worked in the earliest days of Genius Hour, created this Genius Hour Wiki, which is also the home for the #GeniusHour Twitter chat. http://geniushour.wikispaces.com

- Joy Kirr wrote this outstanding reflection when a parent challenged the value of Genius Hour.
  http://geniushour.blogspot.com/2013/01/more-determined-than-ever.html

- When you want to take a deep dive into community advice, the Genius Hour Live Binder contains the contribution of almost 400 teachers. Its creator, Joy Kirr, explains:

"The LiveBinder was created out of pain....Genius Hour had become something I MUST do with my students. I needed to defend it. I needed to find the stories that motivated others to try it. I needed to let parents know just WHY I was using this time in class on a weekly basis.... I began collecting, every day, posts and ideas that people were tweeting out about their own trials and tribulations, creativity, innovation, engagement, passion..."

http://www.livebinders.com/play/play?id=829279

Here are some more, excellent sources of inspiration on Genius Hour:

#Edchat and **#edtechchat** - Join the conversation on Twitter!

Edutopia offers comprehensive coverage on education from both staff writers and top educators: Edutopia.org

EdSurge is an excellent source for cutting edge developments in Ed tech: EdSurge.com

Education Week - Technology is the tech section of one of the education world's biggest information hubs: edweek.org

TeachThought is a "progressive learning brand dedicated to supporting educators in evolving learning for a 21st century audience," TeachThought.com

Why Genius Hour? Helping You Make the Case

When we discuss Genius Hour with teachers who are new to it, we sometimes hear, "This would never fly in my school." But tens of thousands of educators around the world have made the case for launching it in their classrooms. We've reviewed scores of articles with advice on this topic from educators who have been the most successful in launching Genius Hour.

These are some of the recommended strategies:

- **Go in with a Plan** - Use the preparation mentioned above to prove this is a carefully thought out approach to learning. Showing how learning objectives and standards will be met.

- **Show Examples** - There are thousands of teachers in classrooms around the world doing Genius Hour successfully. Find great examples by searching #GeniusHour on Twitter and by checking out The Global Genius Hour wiki and the Genius Hour LiveBinder. http://theglobalgeniushourproject.wikispaces.com http://www.livebinders.com/play/play/829279

- **Connect to the Mission** - Every educator wants to prepare his or her students for future success. Genius Hour is one of the most powerful tools to achieve this, but you may have to make this mission-driven connection clear.

- **Share research** - AJ Juliani offers "The Research Behind 20% Time" a fantastic list of research supporting the benefits of Genius Hour. His post also includes helpful books, links to other teachers' Genius Hour work, and connections to Common Core State Standards. http://ajjuliani.com/research/

Listen to this short BAM! Radio segment on *Three Ways to Get Your School Administrator's Support for Genius Hour*.

http://www.bamradionetwork.com/innovated/1796-three-ways-to-get-your-school-administrators-support-for-genius-hour

Communications With Parents

Once you've convinced your administration, the next step may be "selling" it to your students' parents. Because of a spate of attention recently to genius hour and individualized learning, this may be easier than it would have been five years ago. Here are some of the better letters we've found for introducing parents to genius hour. Bear in mind that none of these teachers had the benefit of this guide; you'll have to customize your letter somewhat to mention the "First 20 Days" approach.

Kevin Brookhouser - "A letter to my students and parents about the 20% Project" http://www.iteachithink.com/2012/08/a-letter-to-my-students-and-parents.html

Kevin's letter to the students and parents of his 10th grade English class walks through each element of their 20% time process. The letter is neatly divided into sections, and it includes helpful videos and links to explain the ideas behind the class's undertaking—particularly his ideas around failure.

Nicole Hill - "Genius Hour Project" Letter

Nicole's letter is similar to Kevin's in that she nods to Dan Pink's *Drive*, Google employees' use of 20% time, and the importance of failure. She clearly outlines that goals for her high school communications class, including its "product focus"—making sure students complete the year with a tangible end product. It includes a structured timeline and assessment.
http://www.dasd.k12.pa.us/cms/lib3/PA01000215/Centricity/Domain/221/Letter%20to%20parents%20and%20students.pdf

Mrs. Helwick and Mrs. Withrow, two Language Arts teachers - this letter is similar to the others, but provides some excellent language to cover the point that Genius Hour is about the process, more than the final product.

http://www.sequimschools.wednet.edu/cms/lib6/WA01000561/Centricity/Domain/319/example%20letter%20to%20parents.pdf

Genius Hour Starter is a free, digital download that includes a parent letter, as well as advice on approaching administrators.

https://www.teacherspayteachers.com/Product/Genius-Hour-Starter-1002142

Must Have Tech Tools

Genius Hour can be done with any group of students in almost any setting. However, having the right technology will enhance your students' ability to get the most out of it.

Technology enables another aspect that all students need highly developed skills in: creative communication. Many of the tools below allow students to share their passion and knowledge through different media. In the same way that Vines and Minecraft have engaged students as creators, Genius Hour is a time for students to express their expertise in new, interactive formats.

Tech Tool	Description
OneNote	A cross-platform, free tool for organization and collaboration. Also, see how you can manage your classroom with OneNote Class Notebook.
Thrively	Thrively is a tool to help students - and their parents and teachers - learn about their strengths and passions.
Twitter	A way for students to connect directly with people who share passions. A tweet can engage professionals on many levels.
Skype	The most widely used video-conferencing software in school. Use it to connect your classroom to the outside world.

Canva	Online design tool for students to create beautiful, professional visuals about their work. The site offers tutorials through their Canva Design School.
YouTube/ Vimeo/ SchoolTube	Easy ways for students to share their videos with the class and beyond.
Weebly	Website builder for students to organize their projects. It is simple to use and has options specifically for students and educators.
Yoursphere	An online space for students to create a group and collaborate around a project. As a COPPA-compliant service, it is especially useful for students under 13.
Kidblog	Blogging platform for students to write and reflect on their learning.
Padlet	Digital bulletin board. Facilitates idea sharing & collaboration.
Sway	Easily create free websites for students to share their Genius Hour Projects with this free tool used to create and share interactive reports, presentations and personal stories.
Docs.com	Publish and share your student's Genius Hour projects with the world with this free tool, Docs.com.
Office Mix	A free add-in for PowerPoint. Everything you need to easily create and share interactive online videos, http://officemix.com
Snip	A visual storytelling tool. With Snip, you can add your own voice, ink and annotations to an image and share it with your friends/co-workers in ways that you can't share screenshots today. http://mix.office.com/snip

Launching and Sustaining Genius Hour

As we explained at the outset, our lessons cover the first 20 days, and are aimed at setting the conditions for a successful launch of Genius Hour.

What do you do on Day 21? Here are answers from some of the better educators we know:

- **Paul Solarz,** a fifth grade teacher in Illinois, offers these step-by-step instructions for creating passion projects, as well as this document with additional resources and some of his students' completed work.

  http://psolarz.weebly.com/mr-solarz-eportfolio/step-by-step directions-for-creating-passion-projects-in-our-classroom

  http://psolarz.weebly.com/2013-2014-passion-projects.html

- **Joy Kirr,** a seventh grade language arts teacher, offers this collection of resources, including her week-by-week guide.

  http://scholarsrm239.weebly.com/what-is-genius-hour.html

https://docs.google.com/document/d/1VnV5soA1rO0xiRtH88IR9_Y
ZSbky4sRjYRl3bIhBF98/edit

- **Jennifer Ward,** a high school teacher in Pennsylvania, imple-
  mented this #HavPassionProject with her students, with
  remarkable results.

  http://www.jenniferward.org/2015/01/anything-really-really.html

- At the 2015 ISTE Conference, **Gallit Zvi** conducted a stellar
  presentation on Genius Hour. Here is a document that collects
  all of the resources and slides that she shared. Denise Krebs created a similar presentation that you can find here.

  https://docs.google.com/document/d/12UBrUrpRLbikIIcYp-
  Q74MxztZkcIlFcgZMbgLbgmFY/edit

  https://docs.google.com/presentation/d/1nCtJKQP0I-
  FX51HAekGom-MY8FJ7iq5Wuf_td-flSm8/edit#slide=id.p

- For advice on dealing with students who are so fixated on the
  "game of school" that they struggle to participate in exploring
  their passion, read "What to Do When Genius Hour Fails" by
  A.J. Juiliani.

  http://ajjuliani.com/genius-hour-fails/

How Do I Grade Genius Hour

Hopefully you have found a few common themes throughout this guide:

- Genius hour is about the process, not the final product.

- All students are unique individuals with the capability to do genius work.

- Every student has particular strengths and passions waiting to be leveraged and explored.

- Collaboration is so much better than competition in preparing students for the modern world and workforce.

With these themes in mind, where do you think we come down on the question of whether or not to "grade" student's participation in genius hour?

Assess the effort, the dedication and diligence, the willingness to participate fully in the lessons and embrace the ideals we've set forth.

But please do not make genius hour the equivalent of the science fair, with a strict rubric and points taken off for failing to precisely complete the rubric, sharp deadlines and cutthroat competition. Most of us know that this leads invariably to procrastination, parents spending money on materials, yelling, and finishing the project while the student cries himself or herself to sleep after midnight.

Not exactly a formula for liberating the genius of our students, is it?

If you set the proper tone from Day 1, and the students learn that their effort and output will be shared with the world, and not just with their teacher, then genius will show up.

Presentations and Sharing

As teachers, we learn to think in terms of assessment and the end game: the quiz at the end of the week, the final exam at the end of the year, the report card that arrives in the summer mail.

As I also discuss in the section on grading, in my opinion, the process is more important than the output, and assessment should measure effort and diligence more than the final product.

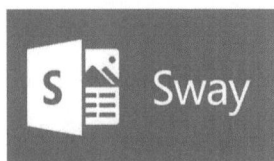

If the process works as it should, then student "output" may be a video documentary, a podcast, a traditional paper, a series of photographs, a work of art, a Sway, or an oral presentation. Or something our imagination can't even conjure up. Some students may decide to embark on a project that will take the full-school year - and perhaps the next one as well. Others may work on a long series of short projects.

Sway is a brand new creation tool from Office joining Word, Excel, PowerPoint and OneNote. Sway helps you easily create and share an interactive web-based canvas of your ideas, which looks great on any platform or device. Teachers can use Sway to create and share interactive lessons, assignments, study guides, trip reports, and best practices. Students can use Sway bring assignments, projects, reports, and study materials to life in a new way.

1. **Sign up** for Sway yourself at **Sway.com**

2. **Get started with this help link**

   https://support.office.com/en-US/article/Getting-Started-with
   Sway-2076C468-63F4-4A89-AE5F-424796714A8A

3. Now you can bring your images in OneNote into Sway for situations like research (**see this blog post for more information**) https://blogs.office.com/2015/03/03/sway-now-lets-add-onenote-images-use-types-web-embeds-share-new-ways/

4. **Learn more** about Sway for Education by visiting **http://aka.ms/SwayIntroductionEducation**.

   Some winning teacher examples from a recent "Sway Your OneNote Love" contest with Microsoft Innovative Educators **See examples** of how other educators and students have been using Sway:

   https://blogs.office.com/2015/01/15/announcing-sway-onenote-love-contest-winners/

   Teacher uses:
   Sharing best practices for using OneNote
   https://sway.com/NbOTamR8Stck0W6O

   Providing supplemental material for a holiday concert program
   https://sway.com/2bS73n8eAFuqhrKM

   Making a field trip study guide
   https://sway.com/2bS73n8eAFuqhrKM

Sharing a class project recap with parents
https://sway.com/6u960qUSjrQmsYzr

Creating an interactive math lesson
https://sway.com/0WDQZ9MXgWcRtczE

Student uses:
Making a class presentation
https://sway.com/WRRb6UIxDZY3-9ea

Publishing a biology report
https://sway.com/9ivWgqoN2DVvUxS8

Creating a portfolio of work
https://sway.com/cFVJVMK8PACd2AOW

Also, some ambitious teachers encourage their students to present their own TED-style talks - and perhaps their very own actual TED Talks.

For support on this:

- Visit Ted-Ed Clubs
  http://ed.ted.com/clubs

- Read "What Students Can Learn From Giving Ted Talks"
  http://ww2.kqed.org/mindshift/2014/11/25/what-students can-learn-from-giving-tedx-talks/

- Visit "The TEDxClassroomProject"
  https://tedxproject.wordpress.com

Liberating Genius – The Next Level: Choose2Matter

Six months after we published "The Passion Driven Classroom," I delivered this talk at TEDxDesMoines, titled "You Matter," in which I discussed something I had notice in my earliest days in the classroom:

The most dangerous thing for any human being is to believe they don't matter.

I spoke of how two words - You Matter - can change lives and change our world, if we understand them and we leverage them in the right way. https://vimeo.com/103280107

People reacted powerfully to this call to action, undertaking awe-inspiring quests to address problems in our world.

Choose2Matter is a universal movement that was created in response to this breathtaking reaction.

Choose2Matter is the intersection of You Matter and Genius Hour.

It begins with a question that helps students explore their passions: "What matters most to you, and why?"

We then take it an evolution further, by asking: "What breaks your heart about that?" and "What are we going to do about it?"

Students have moved beyond learning, to take action that has an impact on the world.

Our first step in fostering the Choose2Matter movement was to write the "You Matter Manifesto" in September 2011. A year later, we collaborated with famed children's author Peter Reynolds on "Make Your Mark That Matters Day," in which we asked students around the world to virtually sign the You Matter Manifesto. We were stunned when 877,000 students from 6 continents did so!

We began to support schools around the world in adopting the "You Matter" message as their theme. Many schools have held special welcome ceremonies on the first day of school, or full day You Matter celebrations during the school year. Some have held parades, while a school in Australia held a flash mob in the town square.

www.youtube.com/watch?v=hw24pCH1UsE&feature=youtu.be

Before long, students began to ask us to visit their school, and Choose2Matter LIVE was born. We held eight trial events, each with great success. At these events:

- Students worked collaboratively to develop innovative solutions to social problems.
- Students acquired the knowledge skills and tools necessary to transform the world.
- We connected students in real-time to adult mentors.
- Students learned the power of learning directly from others.
- Students began to grow into their new role as leaders and engines for social change.

In the wake of these events, we're now bringing Choose2Matter to thousands of schools around the world each year. It is an explosively growing movement that will change the world.

A global movement that seeks to make "mattering" a way of life.

A challenge to **ACCEPT** that you matter - that you have a unique genius. An invitation to **ACCELERATE** the message of you matter to others. An expectation that you will **ACT** to contribute your genius to the world.

This framework empowers people to embrace vulnerability to examine what matters most to them, and why; to consider what breaks their heart about it; and to determine what they can do about it. The process produces fiercely empowered activists and innovators.

There is only one rule: **BE BRAVE**

To participate in Choose2Matter, contact us at
Choose2Matter@Gmail.com

Additional Reading

- *Passion Driven Classroom* by Angela Maiers and Amy Sandoval

- *Classroom Habitudes* by Angela Maiers

- *Drive* by Dan Pink

- *The Genius Hour Guidebook*, by Denise Krebs and Gallit Zvi

- *Inquiry and Innovation: Using 20% Time, Genius Hour, and PBL to Drive Student Success* by A.J. Juliani

- *Finding Your Element* by Ken Robinson

- *Mentoring Student Passions Through Inquiry-Driven Research* - Christina Brennan

- *The 20Time Project: How educators can launch Google's formula for future-ready innovation* by Kevin Brookhouser

- *Pure Genius: Building a Culture of Innovation and Taking 20% Time to the Next Level* by Dan Wettrick

Genius Matters Kit

Please keep an eye out for future announcements of the availability of our "Genius Matters" toolkit. It will be available in the Choose2 Matter Store.

http://www.choose2matter.org/stores/

It will offer a collection of nametags, stickers, certificates, posters and other reproducibles to decorate your classroom and enhance your genius hour experience.

Closing Thoughts

Genius is not a myth.

It is the realization that each and every person on the planet is capable of making one kind of contribution. It is internalizing beautiful truth that we each possess something within us the ability for game changing thinking and the potential to manifest breakthrough ideas that can help us break the chains of mediocrity and stir the best talents within.

So if you think you are willing, ready and brave enough to tap into your five-year-old self, we leave you with one simple question:

Do you believe the following statement?

"You are a GENIUS and the WORLD needs your CONTRIBUTION."
→ANGELA MAIERS

Do you believe it as fiercely as your students believe it? This revolution belongs to everyone. It does not belong to us. It is not yours. It's not even just theirs---it is all of ours.

We all contribute and make it possible. There is no guru, no oracles, no Jedi Masters.

We are just a group of people passionately committed to making our mark on the world. It's everyone's responsibility to grow, share and spread the impact we're creating.

Welcome to Genius Hour.